CHILDREN'S ENCYCLOPEDIA OF HORSES

Claudia Martin

Picture Credits:

Every attempt has been made to clear copyright. Should there be any inadvertent omission, please apply to the publisher for rectification.

Alamy: 5br (Dorling Kindersley Ltd), 8–9 (Zoonar/Helge Schulz), 13tr (Jeronimo Nisa/Associated Press), 24–25, 83tr (Split Second), 30–31, 34–35, 84–85, 94cr, 122–123 (Slawik, C./juniors@wildlife), 36–37, 76l (Juniors Bildarchiv/F315), 38c, 58br (Arco/G. Lacz), 40cl (Ian Lamond), 45bc (Zuma Press), 48–49, 90bl, 94bc (Mark J. Barrett), 50tr (Martin Siepmann/Westend61 GmbH), 52–53 (Martina Berg), 52cl (MBerg/Panther Media GmbH), 58–59, 100–101 (blickwinkel/Lenz), 61cr (Grebler, M./Juniors), 62cl (Renato Valterza), 62bc, 68–69, 76br, 80–81 (Juniors Bildarchiv/F368), 67tr (Galopin), 82–83 (Tierfotoagentur/V. Janosch), 86br (Chris Maddaloni/Associated Press), 97tc (Michele Burgess), 104cr (Allan Wright), 114–115 (Choups), 114br (Germaine Alexakis), 124–125 (Astrid Harrisson), 124bl (Lucy Calder); **Getty Images:** 4–5 (Silke Klewitz-Seemann), 4bl, 25tr (Westend61), 22–23 (Mlenny), 28–29 (CasarsaGuru), 39tc (Cavan Images), 46br (Sven Nackstrand), 62–63 (DEA/B.Langrish), 69cr (Reza), 82bc (De Agostini), 104cl (Ina Fassbender), 111br (Johner Images), 116–117 (Ippei Naoi), 119cr (zhouyousifang), 122c (imageBROKER/Martina Katz); **Science Photo Library:** 7bc (Samantha Elmhurst); **Shutterstock:** 1, 56bc, 78–79, 80cl, 81br (juhipp), 5tl, 95br (Shawn Hamilton), 5tc, 36cr (SeventyFour), 6–7 (PhotocechCZ), 6c (rontav), 6bl (EcoPrint), 7tr (imageBROKER.com), 8cl (spatuletail), 8br (Pecold), 9br (Vladimir Wrangel), 10–11, 11tr (arthorse), 10b, 31tr, 54–55, 121t, 121c (Abramova Kseniya), 11cr (Shot4Sell), 12–13, 12br (Belarmino Essado), 12c1 (Eric Isselee), 12c2 (otsphoto), 12c3+4 (Irina Maksimova), 14–15, 15br, 48br, 50–51, 51br, 112–113 (Annabell Gsoedl), 14c1, 35tr (anjajuli), 14c2 (Oleksii Nedolia), 14c3, 30c (vprotastchik), 14c4 (racorn), 14c5 (savitskaya iryna), 15tr (Tonia Kraakman), 16–17 (Sllittle), 16cl (Anastasija Popover), 16br (onewildlifer), 17br (Invisible Edit), 18–19 (Hugo Martins Oliveira), 18 (zorina larisa), 19t (Liliya Shiapak), 19br (Carol Mauad), 20–21, 105tr, 106–107 (Rita_Kochmarjova), 20c (pfluegler-photo), 20bl (konnik), 21br, 92–93, 120bl, 121br (www.MartinaBurianova.cz), 22cl (Beck Dunn Photography), 22br (Rob Keller), 23tl (Vadim Petrakov), 24cr (Anzhelina), 24bl (Uzo Borewicz), 26–27, 27tr (Juan Carlos Munoz), 26cr (rybarma95), 26br (22 Images Studio), 28c1 (Sari ONeal), 28c2 (Marie Charouzova), 28c3 (Tanja Esser), 28c4 (bmf-foto.de), 28br, 33br (Rolf Dannenberg), 29tl (veronellefoto), 30bl (Osetrik), 32–33, 57br (Azahara Perez), 32cr (Ann Kosolapova), 32bl (BearFotos), 34cl (E. Druz), 34br (bilderfinder), 36bl (Pixel-Shot), 37tr (Warren Price Photography), 38–39, 38br (JM-DigitalPhotography), 40–41 (SandrasKnipserei), 40br (dcurzon), 41tr (Gill Kennett), 42–43 (Dan Baillie), 42bc (Charles Wayne Lytton), 43tc (jo Crebbin), 43br (Kimberly Watley), 44–45 (Vivienstock), 44c (Christine Chantepie), 44br (Gill Davies), 45cr (Makarova Viktoria), 46–47, 46cl (Annelie Carlsson), 47tr (Wirestock Creators), 48c (anakondasp), 49tl (Colin Seddon), 49cr (navatu), 50bl (mRGB), 52br (Nancy Kennedy), 53tc (HixnHix), 54tr (Edoma), 54bl, 64br, 85tr, 86cl, 88–89, 94–95 (olgaru79), 54bc, 92c (Sabine Hagedorn), 55tr, 60br, 74–75, 75br, 96–97 (horsemen), 56–57, 56cl, 80cr (Holly S Cannon), 56cr (Adam Bencsik), 59tc (FastWinn Photography), 58cl (Youness Fakoiallah), 60–61 (Anaite), 60c (RossHelen), 61tc (Lupiphoto), 62cr (Michaelpuche), 63tr (Lilia Becker), 64–65 (zamkniete w migawce), 64c, 65tl (david muscroft), 66–67 (Olesya Nakipova), 66cl, 66br (Daria Koskova), 68cr (Aleksandra Tokarz), 68bc, 71cr (Edoma), 69br (etibarname), 70–71 (Makarova Viktoria), 70c (Julia Shepeleva), 70br, 86–87 (Olga_i), 71tc (Catherine Anne Thomas), 72–73 (Marco Iacobucci Epp), 72cl (Xavier Boudon), 72br (pixinoo), 73tr (slowmotiongli), 74cl, 89cr (Alla-Berlezova), 74bl, 74br (Sirbouman), 76–77, 80br (Nicole Ciscato), 77br (Giadoart), 78bc (Ventura), 79cr (Stuart Litoff), 79br (scrigelova), 80bc (Kwadrat), 83br (Mats Lindberg), 85br (Perry Correll), 87tr (Darya Eraleva), 88c (mveldhuizen), 89tc (Rita_Kochmarjova), 89c (Beatrice Foord-St-Laurent), 89br (Georgia Evans), 90–91 (Pegasene), 90c (Christopher Crosby Morris), 91tr (Casey N), 92cl, 121cr (Vera Zinkova), 92br (Diane Garcia), 93cr (Jana Mackova), 96c (Stephen William Robinson), 96br (Jill Lang), 98–99 (Jess Kraft), 98cl (JeremyRichards), 99br (Daniel San Martin), 100cr (IngeBlessas), 100bl (Jackson Stock Photography), 101tr (Catzatsea), 102–103 (Louis-Michel Desert), 102c (Smiler99), 102br (PIC by Femke), 103tc (Nel727), 104–105 (snapvision), 104br, 107cr (JW.photography31), 106c (Gail Johnson), 106br, 107c (nigel baker photography), 107t (Daisy Shakespeare), 108–109 (Ron van der Stappen), 108cr (Donna Ellen Coleman), 108bl (klauscook), 108br (Magnus Binnerstam), 109tr (Santimila), 110–111 (Myra Wippler), 110cl (Rolf_52), 110br (Istvan Csomortani), 112cl (Olya Muromtseva), 112c (Justin Fotos und Videos), 112br (Femke Ketelaar), 113br (Silaghi Octavian), 114cl (Jane Rix), 115br (Vangelis T), 116cl (skywing-sOO), 116cr (Tooykrub), 116bl (LeeSensei), 116br (hika-j), 117tr (BluePacificMedia), 118–119 (Khodchenko Sergii), 118bc (tbbstudio), 119br (outcast85), 120–121 (KimBiranda), 122br (Vibe Images), 123tl (Grezova Olga), 125tr (Janelle Lugge), 125c (jimmonkphotography), 125br (aleigha blakley);
Wikimedia Commons: 84bl (Thomas Springer), 94tr (Heather Moreton from Louisville, KY, USA), 94cl (AkimaDoll), 98br (Harvey Barrison).
Jacket: Front cover all Shutterstock: main image Anzhelina, l Rita_Kochmarjova, cl PHOENIX1423, c Shutterstock, cr CW Pix, r Makarova Viktoria. Back cover: Lorraine Inglis. Front flap: Shuttertock Donna Ellen Coleman. Back flap: Shutterstock Lucia Pinto.

ARCTURUS

This edition published in 2026 by Arcturus Publishing Limited
26/27 Bickels Yard, 151–153 Bermondsey Street,
London SE1 3HA

ISBN: 978-1-3988-5730-8
CH012452US
Supplier 29, Date 1025, PI00011093

Printed in China

Author: Claudia Martin
Consultant: Nicola Jane Swinney
Designer: Lorraine Inglis
Picture researcher: Paul Futcher
Editor: Becca Clunes
Design manager: Jessica Holliland
Managing editor: Joe Harris

CONTENTS

The World of Horses 4

Chapter 1: Horse Life 6

Living with Humans 8
Conformation 10
Gaits 12
Senses 14
Communication 16
Coats 18
Mares and Foals 20
Feral Horses 22
Sports 24

Chapter 2: Horse Care 26

Grooming 28
Diet 30
Stables 32
Pasture 34
Health 36

Chapter 3: Heavy Horses 38

Shire 40
Clydesdale 42
Percheron 44
North Swedish 46
Brabant 48
Noriker 50
American Cream Draft 52

Chapter 4: Light Horses 54

Arabian 56
Barb 58
Thoroughbred 60
Cleveland Bay 62
Gypsy Vanner 64
Marwari 66
Karabakh 68
Orlov Trotter 70
Selle Français 72
Andalusian 74
Maremmano 76
Lipizzaner 78
Frederiksborger 80
Swedish Warmblood 82
Oldenburger 84
Holsteiner 86
Appaloosa 88
Morgan 90
American Paint 92
Rocky Mountain 94
Paso Fino 96
Peruvian Paso 98
Australian Stock Horse 100

Chapter 5: Ponies 102

Shetland Pony 104
Welsh Mountain Pony 106
Icelandic Horse 108
Gotland Pony 110
Fjord Horse 112
Skyros Pony 114
Yonaguni 116
Tibetan Pony 118
American Miniature Horse 120
Falabella 122
Australian Pony 124

GLOSSARY 126

INDEX 128

The World of Horses

Around 60 million horses are grazing and galloping across the world. These horses range in size from huge, strong Shire horses to Falabellas too tiny to be ridden. While some horses wander in the wild, others are in training for driving or dressage competitions.

The Wielkopolski is a light horse that was bred in Poland.

The Wielkopolski is athletic and highly trainable. It excels at show jumping, dressage, and eventing.

Loved Horses

Humans have had a long relationship with horses. Over the last 5,500 years, horses have helped us with transportation, farming, and warfare. Today, some horses are still hard at work in jobs from movie-making to policing. Yet, most modern horses get their exercise from being ridden for fun. Over all these years, two important facts have stayed true: humans have loved their horses—and horses have loved their kind owners!

Today, some horses work as therapy animals. These gentle horses offer rides and friendship.

Beautiful Breeds

There are around 300 breeds of horse, each of them developed by humans to have a particular appearance, abilities, and personality. The world's breeds are often divided into three groups: heavy horses, which are suited to pulling loads; light horses, which are ideal for riding and sports; and the smallest breeds, called ponies, which are often suited to children.

The Canadian warmblood is among North America's most popular breeds of light horse. It is suited to riding, dressage, and show jumping.

Many horses, like the one shown here, do not belong to a breed, because their ancestors are unknown or are from several breeds. Often called a grade horse, a non-breed horse may be less expensive to buy, but it is just as lovable!

This breed is 15.2–16.2 hands (157–168 cm; 62–66 in) high at the withers.

Hands High

A horse's height is measured from the ground to the highest point of its withers. The withers are the ridge between a horse's shoulder blades. Traditionally, the measurement is given in hands, which are based on the width of a human hand. One hand is equal to 4 inches (around 10 cm), so 15 hands is 60 inches (4 x 15). If a horse's height is not an exact number of hands, a decimal point is used: 15 hands and 1 inch (61 inches) is written as 15.1, 15 hands and 2 inches is 15.2, and 15 hands and 3 inches is 15.3. In this book, each breed's height is given in hands, centimeters, and inches to its withers.

A horse's height is measured to the withers, using a tall stick with a sliding horizontal arm.

Chapter 1

Horse Life

Along with humans, dogs, and lions, horses belong to a big group of animals called mammals. Like most mammals, horses have four legs, grow hair, and feed their young on milk. Horses are in a group of plant-eating, hoofed mammals known as the horse family.

Found in Central Asia, Przewalski's horse is the only truly wild horse that is still alive today.

Horse Family

There are seven species in the horse family. A species is a group of animals that look similar and can make babies together. The horse family holds three species of asses and three species of zebras. The seventh species is the wild horse, which is divided into two smaller groups called subspecies: Przewalksi's horse and the domestic horse, which is the subspecies that contains the horses that humans ride. The two subspecies can make babies together, but they look a little different from each other.

Like other asses, the African wild ass has long ears, an upright-growing mane, and a tail that ends with a tuft. The domestic donkey is a descendant of this ass.

Like all zebras, the plains zebra has black and white stripes. It has an upright-growing mane and a tuft at the end of its tail.

DID YOU KNOW? Horses became extinct in the Americas around 10,000 years ago, possibly due to climate change and hunting by humans.

PRZEWALSKI'S HORSE

Height: 12–14 hands (122–142 cm; 48–56 in)
Lifespan: 20–25 years
Origin: Central Asia
Coat: Dun with a dark dorsal stripe (down the middle of the back) and paler on the muzzle and belly
Uses: Grazing on grassland, which helps to maintain the habitat and prevent wildfires
Personality: Shy of humans, but loyal and gentle with its herd

This subspecies has an upright-growing mane and is shorter and stockier than the domestic horse.

THE HOOF
1. Tendons attach to the leg muscles.
2. Toe bones
3. The "digital cushion" absorbs shock to protect the foot's bones and soft tissues.
4. The hoof wall is made from keratin, the same material as horns and nails.

Przewalski's horse is a cousin of the domestic horse: The two subspecies share an ancestor that lived more than 38,000 years ago.

Hoofed Family

The horse family evolved in North America around 54 million years ago. Early horses were a little different from modern ones: They were smaller, had three or four toes, and ate leaves from forest trees. Over time, horses grew larger and lost their side toes, developing just one toe with a tough wall—called a hoof—which allows a heavy animal to run fast on any ground. Horses moved to open plains, where they grazed on grasses. Then horses walked to Asia, which was linked to America by a strip of land, and walked on to Europe and Africa.

Living with Humans

The Heck horse was bred by the Heck brothers in a German zoo in the 1930s.

Around 5,500 years ago, humans first captured wild horses and began to domesticate them, by taming and training them. We also began to change the way horses looked and behaved, by choosing which horses to breed with each other.

Domestication

Wild horses were first domesticated on the grasslands of Central Asia. All of today's domestic horses are descended from Central Asian and European wild horses. Those wild horse species became extinct as domestic horses were spread far and wide by humans. Asian and European domestic horses were taken to Africa, then across the oceans to the Americas and Australia.

Cave paintings give us an idea of how the ancestors of the domestic horse looked. This painting of a European wild horse was made more than 17,000 years ago at Lascaux, in France. The horse looks a little like a Przewalski's horse, with a dun coat, upright-growing mane, thick neck, and short legs.

Selective Breeding

For thousands of years, humans have selected which horses would be allowed to breed. By choosing only strong, tall, gentle, or fast horses, horse-owners could pass on those characteristics to foals. By selective breeding over generations, owners created horse breeds with different characteristics. From around the 14th century, some owners kept records of their horses' pedigrees (the names of their parents and grandparents), creating breed registries, also called studbooks. Today, all "purebred" horses are recorded in a breed registry.

The Kladruber horse was bred in Czechia to have strength and elegance for pulling carriages. The first Kladruber studbook was created in the 16th century, making it Czechia's oldest registered breed.

HECK

Height: 12.2–13.2 hands (127–137 cm; 50–54 in)
Lifespan: 25–30 years
Origin: Germany
Coat: Dun with a dark dorsal stripe
Uses: Riding and light driving
Personality: Gentle and friendly, but independent-minded

DID YOU KNOW? Established breeds usually have a "closed" studbook, which means that only registered horses of that breed can be used for breeding.

Conformation

A horse's conformation is its body shape, proportions, and muscling. Different conformations are suited to different work. Whether a horse's conformation is elegant or sturdy, all horses have around 205 bones and 700 muscles.

The Akhal-Teke is famed for its beautiful conformation and the metallic shine of its coat.

Conformation Basics

Although ponies and heavy horses often have a stockier conformation, light horses usually follow these conformation guidelines. For balance, their neck length (from poll to mid-shoulder) should be 1.5 times the head length (from muzzle to poll). An ideal body shape is "square," which means that the height from the withers to the ground is equal to the body length.

This Russian Don horse has excellent conformation. The slope of its shoulder (running from the point of the shoulder to the highest point of the withers) is around 45 degrees, which allows a long stride.

AKHAL-TEKE

Height: 14.1–15.3 hands (145–160 cm; 57–63 in)
Lifespan: 20–30 years
Origin: Turkmenistan
Coat: Usually bay, buckskin (pictured), chestnut, gray, or black, all with a metallic shine
Uses: Dressage, show jumping, eventing, racing, and endurance riding
Personality: Intelligent, spirited, and too strong-minded for beginner or nervous riders

In the Akhal-Teke, the length of the front leg equals the neck length, allowing balanced movement. The neck is set high on the horse's body, giving plenty of room for the lungs in the chest. Unlike many light horses, the Akhal-Teke has a nearly straight neck, not an arched neck in which the crest curves upward in a gentle arch.

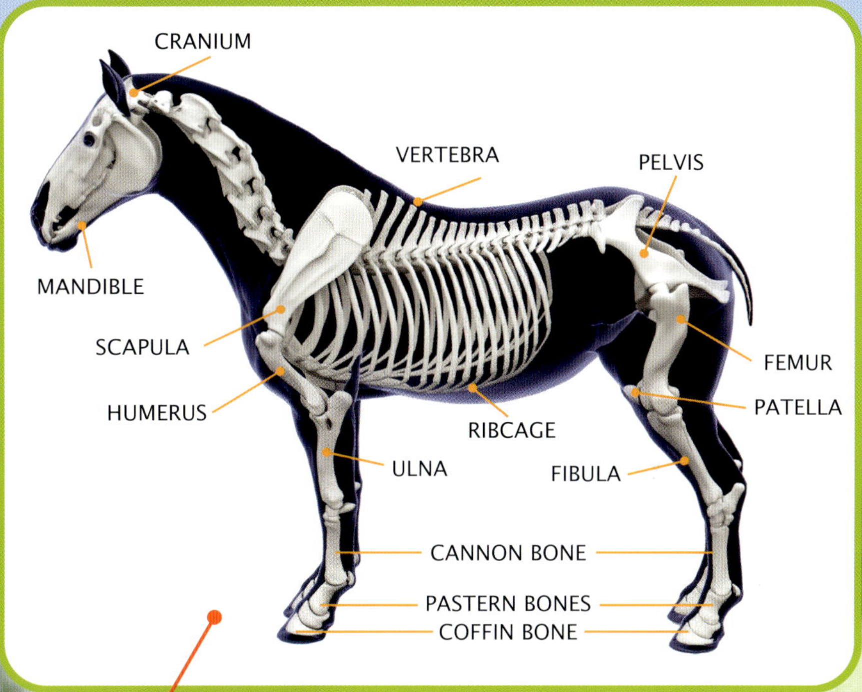

CRANIUM
VERTEBRA
PELVIS
MANDIBLE
SCAPULA
FEMUR
PATELLA
HUMERUS
RIBCAGE
ULNA
FIBULA
CANNON BONE
PASTERN BONES
COFFIN BONE

Each back leg is made up of 19 bones, while each front leg has 20 bones.

In this breed, the tail is high set (on a level with the top of the back)—along with the mane—is sparsely haired.

Skeleton

A horse's skeleton accounts for about 12 percent of its body weight. The heaviest bones are the femurs, which help to create and bear the powerful forces in the horse's hindquarters and back legs.

DID YOU KNOW? From the front, you should be able to trace a straight line down the middle of each of a horse's front legs, while the same is true of the back legs if seen from behind.

Gaits

Horses use different gaits—or patterns of leg movement—as they travel. Most horses have four gaits, with increasing speed: walk, trot, canter, and gallop. However, more than 30 breeds are gaited, which means they can naturally perform a gait other than the standard four.

Four Gaits

Walk: Averaging 7 km/h (4.3 mph), this gait has this footfall pattern: left hind leg, left front leg, right hind leg, right front leg. It is a four-beat gait with an even 1-2-3-4 beat.	
Trot: Averaging 13 km/h (8 mph), the trot can be maintained over longer distances than a canter or gallop. It is a two-beat gait with the footfall pattern: left front with right hind, then right front with left hind.	
Canter: Averaging 21 km/h (13 mph), the canter is a three-beat gait. The footfall pattern depends on the side that the horse leads with, but may be: left hind, right hind with left front, then right front.	
Gallop: Averaging 44 km/h (27 mph), this is a four-beat gait with a footfall pattern that depends on the side that the horse leads with, but may be: right hind, left hind, right front, left front.	

The Mangalarga marchador is the national horse breed of Brazil.

MANGALARGA MARCHADOR

Height: 14.1–15.2 hands (145–158 cm; 57–62 in)
Lifespan: 25–30 years
Origin: Brazil
Coat: Bay, chestnut, gray, black, buckskin, palomino, and pinto
Uses: Ranch work, endurance riding, dressage, and show jumping
Personality: Calm, easy to train, and friendly

Other Gaits

A few horses, such as the Standardbred (see page 71), can perform a gait called a pace instead of a trot. Faster than a trot, a pace is a two-beat gait with the footfall pattern left front with left hind, right front with right hind. Many horses bred in mountainous or remote areas have an ambling gait, which is a four-beat gait that is faster than a walk but usually slower than a canter. The extra footfalls make a journey smoother for a rider than the bouncing trot.

The breed performs a supremely smooth ambling gait called the *marcha picada* ("light-touch gait" in Portuguese).

Bred in the US state of Alabama, the racking horse can perform an ambling gait called the rack at up to 48 km/h (30 mph). The footfall pattern is left hind, left front, right hind, right front.

The *marcha picada* has the footfall pattern of left hind, left front, right hind, right front, with a 1-2, 3-4 beat.

DID YOU KNOW? In most gaited horse breeds, the ability to perform a pace or ambling gait is passed from parent to child in biological instructions called genes.

Senses

In the wild, horses were prey for animals from wolves to bears. As a result, horse senses are tuned to keep them safe. They have the same five senses as humans—smell, sight, hearing, touch, and taste.

Five Senses

Smell: A horse has a stronger sense of smell than a human. It often uses smell first when investigating a new object or person, by blowing out to clear its nose before taking a deep sniff. It recognizes friends by their scent.

Sight: With an eye on either side of its head, a horse can watch all around for danger but cannot see a space in front of its face or under its nose, so give it time to judge obstacles. Although a horse can see colors, some—such as red and orange—cannot be told apart.

Hearing: A horse has excellent hearing due to the funnel shapes of its pinnae (outer ears), which capture sound waves. Moving together or alone, each pinna can be turned in a semi-circle to home in on noises.

Touch: This is a powerful and emotional sense for a horse, allowing it to be calmed by kindly touch from humans and other horses. A horse's most sensitive areas are its face and neck.

Taste: A horse's tongue and mouth can taste the quality, freshness, and nutrients of food, so it will sort through forage to find exactly what it needs.

DID YOU KNOW? A horse's pupils (the black holes that let light into the eye) are horizontal ovals, a shape that helps with seeing movement along the horizon.

Wonderful Whiskers

Also known as sensory hairs, a horse's whiskers—along with sensitive hairs around its eyes and inner ears—are equipped with nerves that are sensitive to touch and air movements. Never trim the sensory hairs, as this prevents a horse from judging distance and can cause confusion and injury.

Like most horses, the Kinsky usually has dark brown irises.

Although it was once routine to remove or cut horse whiskers, whisker-trimming is now banned in several countries and by the International Federation of Equestrian Sports.

KINSKY

Height: 15.2–17 hands (157–173 cm; 62–68 in)
Lifespan: 25–30 years
Origin: Czechia
Coat: Usually golden-yellow, but may be bay, chestnut, or black
Uses: Dressage, show jumping, eventing, riding, racing, police work, and horse-assisted therapy
Personality: Even-tempered, friendly, and smart

Communication

Horses communicate with each other—and with you—using body language, facial expressions, and actions. Although horses do use sounds to show their feelings, they have evolved to limit loud noises that could attract predators.

Communicating with You

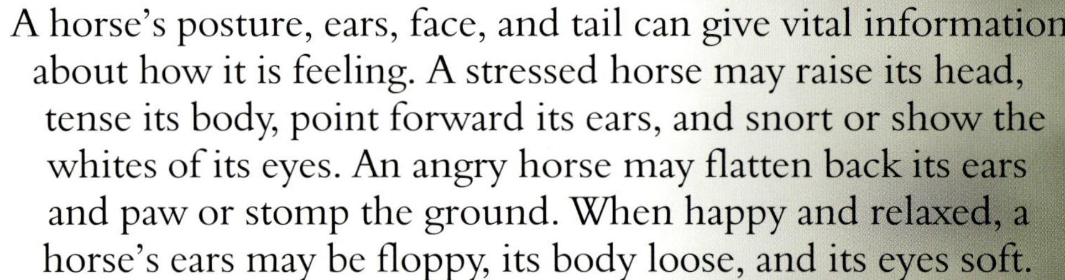

A horse's posture, ears, face, and tail can give vital information about how it is feeling. A stressed horse may raise its head, tense its body, point forward its ears, and snort or show the whites of its eyes. An angry horse may flatten back its ears and paw or stomp the ground. When happy and relaxed, a horse's ears may be floppy, its body loose, and its eyes soft.

A happy horse may gently swing its tail, but a stressed or angry horse may carry its tail high and sharply swish it.

Communicating with Each Other

When greeting another horse, a horse may give a loud sniff or a gentle, high-pitched neigh called a whinny. To show affection, a horse may give a nicker, which is a breathy whinny. A gentle nuzzle might signal that a horse wants grooming or company. If threatened by another horse, a horse may show aggression with tense body language, nudging, or even biting and kicking. However, horses—particularly young ones—often harmlessly play-fight by chasing, rearing, and nipping.

Play-fighting is a way to have fun, learn survival skills, and establish a position in the herd.

DID YOU KNOW? Stallions may pee and poop along their fence line or at the gate, to show other horses the boundary of their "territory."

In each herd, some horses are more dominant, with a higher position in the group. These high-ranking horses start more grooming sessions, which helps to build trust with other horses and to reduce tension.

NEW FOREST PONY

Height: 12-14.2 hands (122-147 cm; 48-58 in)
Lifespan: 25-35 years
Origin: England
Coat: Usually bay, chestnut, or gray
Uses: Some are semi-feral (see page 23), but others are used for riding, show jumping, and dressage
Personality: Kind, calm, and willing to give anything a try

Coats

A horse's coat protects its skin from cold, sunlight, rain, and insects. The length and thickness of the hairs depends on the breed and the season. The coat's color and pattern are passed down from a horse's parents in biological instructions called genes.

The Pampa horse is always pinto, with large white patches on any darker base coat.

Common Coats

Horse hairs get their color from two chemicals called pigments: pheomelanin, which makes a reddish-brown called chestnut; and eumelanin, which makes black. All other coats are made by genes that modify these colors: by changing the color of the points (mane, tail, lower legs, and ear rims); by diluting the coat (making it paler); by adding white markings (where areas of hair have lost their pigment); or by adding white hairs throughout. Here are some common coats:

	**Chestnut:** Also called sorrel, this is a very common coat.		**Palomino:** A chestnut coat with a cream dilution gene is yellow-tan with flaxen points.
	**Black:** This pure coat is relatively uncommon.		**Buckskin:** A bay coat with a cream dilution gene is yellow-cream with black points.
	**Bay:** A bay horse is reddish to dark brown with black points.		**Dun:** The dun dilution gene can act on any base coat, creating gold to gray coats with darker markings, including a dorsal stripe (along the back).
	**Gray:** A gray horse is born any shade, but its hairs gradually turn white over time.		**Spotted:** The leopard gene creates spotting patterns on any base coat.
	**Roan:** From birth, a roan horse has a scattering of white hairs in its base coat.		**Pinto:** Also known as particolored or piebald, a pinto horse has large patches of white over any base coat.

White Markings

Many horses—even those with a solid base coat—have white markings, particularly on the face and lower legs. Here are the most common patterns:

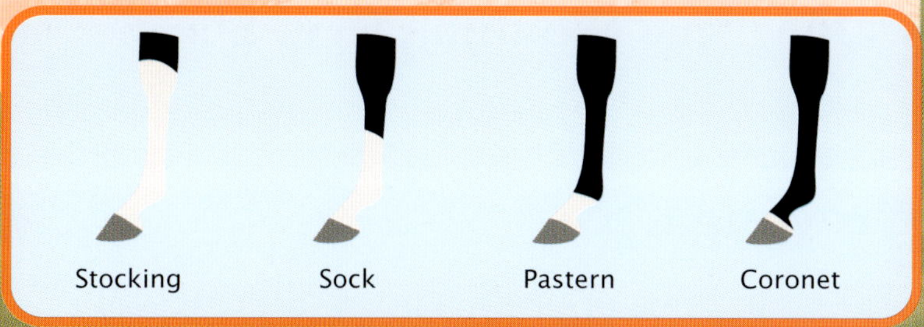

Stocking

Sock

Pastern

Coronet

The Pampa is a "color breed," which means that only horses with a particular coat can be registered.

The founder of this breed, Rafael Tobias de Aguiar, gave his name to a particular pinto pattern called tobiano: rounded white patches on any darker base coat, with white lower legs, white across the top of the back, and a dark head that often has a white star or blaze.

PAMPA

Height: 13.3–14.3 hands (140–150 cm; 55–59 in)
Lifespan: 25–30 years
Origin: Brazil
Coat: Pinto (often in the tobiano pattern) with any darker base coat
Uses: Pleasure and endurance riding, ranch work, and polo
Personality: Loyal, easy to train, and brave

DID YOU KNOW? Most horses have a thicker winter coat that they shed as the days lengthen and temperatures rise in spring.

Mares and Foals

A mare usually gives birth to one foal at a time, after a pregnancy of around 11 months. She will greet her newborn by licking, sniffing, and breathing on it. She may call to her foal with a nicker.

Growing Up

Within an hour of birth, a newborn foal will be able to stand, then take a few shaky steps to drink its mother's milk. After around a week, a foal will nibble on grass, even though all its nutritional needs are met by milk for the first two or three months. At four to seven months old, a foal will stop drinking milk. Most horses are mature enough to be ridden when they are between three and four years old. However, their bones and muscles continue to develop until the age of six or older.

A mare licks clean her newborn foal. At this stage, never step between a mare and her foal.

A foal that is still drinking milk is often called a suckling.

All in the Names

A young horse of either sex is called a foal until it reaches one year old, then it is called a yearling until it reaches two. The special name for a female horse under the age of four is a filly, while a male of the same age is a colt. A female horse of four and older is a mare, while a male horse can be either a stallion or a gelding. A gelding has been "gelded," which means it cannot father foals.

DID YOU KNOW? Most horses live for 25-30 years, but the oldest known horse—a heavy horse named Old Billy—reached the age of 62.

KNABSTRUPPER

Height: 15.1–16 hands (154–162 cm; 61–64 in)
Lifespan: 25–30 years
Origin: Denmark
Coat: Any except gray, palomino, and pinto, but it is often spotted
Uses: Riding, dressage, show jumping, eventing, driving, and equestrian vaulting
Personality: Easy-going, friendly, and obliging

This Knabstrupper mare is staying close to her foal, which she will protect until it is old enough to graze alone.

A foal may hide behind its mother if it sees something new or startling.

For the first month of a foal's life, it will play only with and around its mother. As it gets older, a foal will start to play with other foals and people.

Feral Horses

Many herds of feral horses are galloping free in the wild. Unlike wild animals, which have never been domesticated, feral horses are domestic horses that have strayed or escaped.

Brumbies

Australia has the world's largest population of feral horses, estimated at about 400,000. Called brumbies, these horses are descendants of escaped horses, the first of them belonging to European settlers from the early 19th century. Sometimes, brumbies are rounded up and tamed, becoming riding horses, stock horses, and even show horses.

Adult brumbies have no predators in Australia, so the only threats to their well-being are drought, poisonous plants, and parasites.

Mustangs are feral horses of the western United States.

MUSTANG

Height: Usually 14–15 hands (142–152 cm; 56–60 in)
Lifespan: 15–20 years in the wild; 25–30 years if domesticated
Origin: United States
Coat: Any
Uses: Trail riding, ranch work, rodeo, dressage, and show jumping if domesticated
Personality: Wild and independent if feral; gentle if domesticated

Camargue Horses

The Camargue horse is an ancient French breed known for its sturdy build and gray coat. Herds of Camargue horses live semi-feral in the wetlands of the Camargue region. A semi-feral horse is one that roams freely but is managed and given veterinary care by humans. Semi-feral Camargues are owned and ridden by cattle-herders called *gardians*, but other members of the breed are kept as pets across the world.

DID YOU KNOW? The name "mustang" may come from the old Spanish word *mesteño*, which referred to an animal with no owner.

Sports

Horses are ridden and driven in a wide range of equestrian sports. Over the centuries, different horse breeds have been developed to excel at particular sports. However, in any equestrian sport, the safety of horse and rider must come first.

This chestnut Westphalian stallion is named Aquamarin.

Riding

Highly skilled sports such as dressage and show jumping grew from the training given to war horses. Popular with children, gymkhana is a more relaxed sport involving games of speed and skill on horseback. Horse racing includes flat racing, with short races; jump racing, in which horses race over jumps; and endurance, with races usually over 80 km (50 miles). However, animal welfare groups are concerned about the pressure put on some sport horses and about the safety of horses used in racing and team sports such as polo. Ask a veterinarian for advice before taking part in a sport.

For any sport, always wear a safety helmet, riding boots with a grippy sole, jodhpurs to stay comfortable and secure in the saddle, gloves to prevent blisters from the reins, and a body protector to absorb the shock of a fall or kick.

Driving

Driving sports involve a single horse, pair, or team pulling a vehicle. In harness racing, horses race at a specified gait—a trot or pace—as they pull a two-wheeled cart. Scurry driving is a race in which ponies are driven around a course of cones. In pleasure driving, carriage driving, and fine harness, the emphasis is on manners or style rather than speed.

A combined driving competition has three phases: dressage, cross-country marathon, and obstacle cone driving (pictured).

DID YOU KNOW? The national sport of Afghanistan is *buzkashi*, in which teams of horseriders try to place a goatskin in a goal.

WESTPHALIAN

Height: 15.2–17.2 hands (157–178 cm; 62–70 in)
Lifespan: 25–30 years
Origin: Germany
Coat: Usually bay, chestnut, gray, and black
Uses: Dressage, show jumping, hunter competitions, and riding
Personality: Spirited and brave, yet easy to work with

The Swiss Olympic medal-winner Christine Stückelberger competes at dressage.

Several Westphalian horses have won Olympic medals for their riders in dressage and show jumping.

Chapter 2

Horse Care

Caring for a horse is wonderful, but is also a great long-term responsibility. Every day, a horse needs to have its physical needs met, from hoof care to good food. Just as important are a horse's emotional needs, including love, respect, and time for fun.

Hoof Care

Horse care starts with hoof care! Every day, check hooves for cracks and cuts, then use a hoof pick to remove dirt and stones. Examine shoes for signs of wear and raised nails. Register your horse with a specialist in hoof care, called a farrier, who will probably trim the hoof walls (the hard, outer layer of each hoof) and reshoe every four to six weeks. Not all horses wear shoes, but many do to protect their hooves. A farrier nails a shoe, often made of steel, through the hoof wall—which, like fingernails, cannot feel pain.

To pick out hooves, make sure the horse is safely tied or held. Warn the horse that you are going to pick up a hoof, by first running your hand down its leg. Move the pick from heel to toe, taking care around the sensitive frog (the triangular mound on the bottom of the foot) and facing the pick's sharp end away from your own body.

Drinking Water

The average horse needs to drink at least three or four buckets (30–40 liters; 8–10 US gallons) of fresh, clean water every day. Just like a human body, a horse's body needs plenty of water to run smoothly, as it is the main ingredient in blood and pee. Since water is also in sweat, drinking helps a horse to cool down in hot weather.

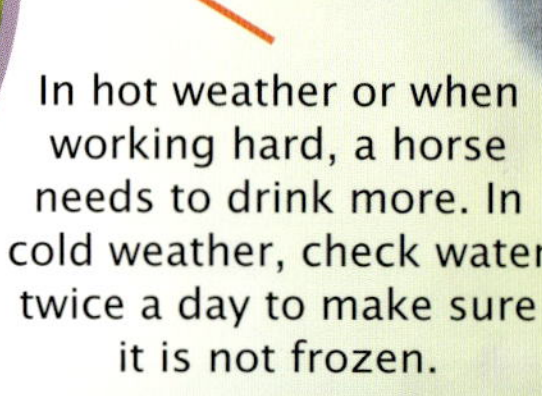

In hot weather or when working hard, a horse needs to drink more. In cold weather, check water twice a day to make sure it is not frozen.

SORRAIA

Height: 14.1–14.3 hands (145–150 cm; 57–59 in)
Lifespan: 25–30 years
Origin: Portugal
Coat: Dun with dark markings
Uses: Ranch work, riding, dressage, and light driving
Personality: Hardy, calm, and reliable, but may prefer to be ridden by one loved person in particular

DID YOU KNOW? A horse's hoof walls grow continuously, at a speed of around 0.6–1 cm (0.2–0.4 in) each month.

Grooming

Grooming keeps a horse's coat and skin in good condition. A grooming session not only removes dirt and knots, but also releases the horse's own natural oils and increases blood flow to the skin.

How to Groom

Before starting to groom, tie the horse loosely—so it can be untied quickly if it becomes restless—to a beam or fence post. Then follow these steps:

Grooming is the perfect opportunity to bond with your horse and to build trust.

	1. Use a soft curry comb (with short rubber bristles) to loosen dirt from the coat, using a circular motion. Do not use a curry comb on the mane, tail, head, and lower legs, as they are too sensitive.	2. Using a dandy brush (with long, stiff bristles), make gentle flicking motions on the horse's body to sweep away the dirt raised by the curry comb.	
	3. With a soft body brush (with medium-length bristles), use long strokes to smooth out the hair. The body brush can also be used gently on the head and legs.	4. Remove any tangles from the mane and tail using your fingers, then brush using a wide-toothed comb.	

HAFLINGER

Height: 13.2–15 hands (137–152 cm; 54–60 in)
Lifespan: 25–35 years
Origin: Austria and northern Italy
Coat: Chestnut with flaxen mane and tail
Uses: Riding, children's dressage and show jumping, light driving, and horse-assisted therapy
Personality: Friendly, easy-going, and calm, making it well suited to children

How Often?

On average, most horses need to be groomed at least once a week. Yet a horse may need grooming more or less often, depending on its coat, activity, the season, and whether it is being groomed by other horses. A horse needs washing with water and shampoo only when necessary. While some horses need washing only a few times a year, others are washed more often because they get muddy.

A horse should not be washed too often, as it strips away natural oils from the coat.

The Haflinger is known for its long, thick, flaxen mane, which needs frequent detangling and gentle brushing.

Since horses enjoy grooming each other in the wild, most horses find grooming very relaxing.

DID YOU KNOW? Signs that a horse is uncomfortable when grooming include pawing the ground, flicking the tail, and flattening the ears.

Diet

Just like humans, horses need a healthy diet so that their body has energy and the materials needed for repair and growth. In the wild, horses munch on grasses, seeds, and other eatable plant parts. Domestic horses are happiest with a similar diet.

A highly successful sport horse, the Trakehner can be rewarded for hard work with a treat, petting, and kind words.

What Food?

The majority of a horse's food should be forage, which is all the plants it would eat if grazing in the wild. Forage includes grass, hay, and haylage. Since a horse's stomach is quite small, it is happiest to nibble at hay, or graze in a safe pasture, throughout the day. If a horse is growing, pregnant, elderly, or working hard, it will need extra energy or vitamins. A veterinarian can advise on giving grain-based concentrates or vitamin-rich supplements.

This Budyonny horse is plucking hay from a net. When placed at a safe and comfortable height, a hay net encourages a horse to feed slowly, as if it is grazing.

It is difficult to know how much your horse is eating when grazing, so ask your vet to check its weight.

How Much Food?

Every day, the average horse needs to eat around 1.5 to 2.5 percent of its body weight in food. This means that, if a horse weighs 500 kg (1,100 lb), it needs about 10 kg (22 lb) of food. Yet every horse should have regular weight checks by a veterinarian to make sure it is eating the right amount for its age and level of activity.

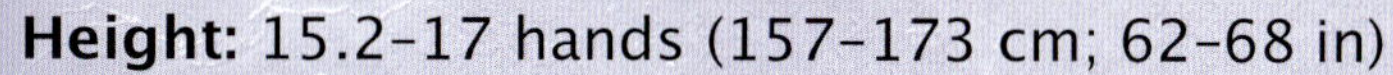

TRAKEHNER

Height: 15.2–17 hands (157–173 cm; 62–68 in)
Lifespan: 25–30 years
Origin: Russia
Coat: Bay, chestnut, gray, and black
Uses: Dressage, show jumping, eventing, and riding
Personality: Trainable, intelligent, and a little more spirited than other warmbloods (see page 54)

Do not give your horse sugary treats, potatoes, tomatoes, turnips, cabbages, fruits with stones, garden waste, or moldy or dusty hay.

A carrot is the perfect healthy treat, but do not give more than one or two carrots or one apple each day.

DID YOU KNOW? To make sure a horse has time to digest its food comfortably, do not feed an hour before or after exercise.

Stables

Every horse needs a safe, comfortable stable where it is protected from the weather. Yet a horse should be kept in its stable for as few of the daylight hours as possible, returning to it only when the needs for exercise and freedom have been met.

Stable Design

Horses are herd animals, so they need to be with other horses as much as possible. Some horses enjoy living in a shared barn, although more nervous animals may prefer their own space. In most stables, horses are housed in separate stalls called loose boxes, which should be positioned so each horse can see and interact with friends. Each horse's loose box—or its space in a shared barn—should be at least 3 m by 3 m (10 ft by 10 ft) for a pony, rising to 3.65 m by 3.65 m (12 ft by 12 ft) for an average-sized horse.

A stable needs plenty of natural light. Air should be able to flow through freely so that horses can breathe fresh, dust-free air.

A horse's bedding will soak up pee and poop, so it should be changed every day.

Stable Needs

Bedding—of straw, wood shavings, or shredded paper—should be placed on the floor for added warmth and comfort. Each loose box should contain water and food. To stop your horse from becoming bored, you could add a horse-safe mirror, scratching mat, or treat ball toy, which releases food when nudged.

DID YOU KNOW? Horses sleep while standing up or lying down. They sleep for short periods that add up to 5-7 hours in total per day.

FREIBERGER

Height: 14.2-15.2 hands (147-157 cm; 58-62 in)
Lifespan: 25-30 years
Origin: Switzerland
Coat: Bay and chestnut
Uses: Riding, driving, and horse-assisted therapy
Personality: Determined, sensible, gentle, and sure-footed on mountain terrain

Pasture

Horses love to wander in a pasture during the day. This allows them to graze freely, which is ideal for their physical health. If they can be turned out with other horses, pasture-time also gives them an essential chance to socialize.

Essential Exercise

Horses need lots of exercise to stay physically and mentally healthy. In the wild, horses walk or run for much of the day. This is why being "turned out" to pasture is essential daily exercise for every domestic horse. It is best for horses to be turned out in groups, which will encourage them to stay active.

If a horse is playing with its "herd" on the pasture all day—like these Clydesdale horses—it may not need to also be ridden every day.

Safe Pasture

Make sure your horse's pasture is secure by checking that its fences are sturdy. Each field should have a separate water supply, which should not usually be a stream, river, or pond due to the risk of pollution. There should also be shelter—either human-made or trees and hedges—for protection from sun and bad weather. Check for rabbit holes, which could cause trips, and remove plants that are harmful to horses, such as ragwort, privet, and oak.

Ensure that fruit trees do not overhang the pasture, as your horse will probably eat too many of these sugary treats!

DID YOU KNOW? In the wild, horses usually wander 20–30 km (12–18 miles) per day in search of food and water.

BLACK FOREST

Height: 14.2–15.3 hands (148–160 cm; 58–63 in)
Lifespan: 25–30 years
Origin: Germany
Coat: Chestnut with flaxen mane and tail
Uses: Driving, riding, and farm work
Personality: Lively, good-tempered, and very agreeable

Bred as a farm horse, the Black Forest horse always has a chestnut coat and flaxen mane and tail.

The ideal pasture is a mixture of low-sugar grasses—such as smooth meadow-grass and sheep's fescue—along with nutritious plants including dandelion and chicory.

When deciding on pasture size, a minimum of 4,000 sq m (43,000 sq ft) is needed per horse—so 10 horses require a pasture of at least 200 by 200 m (655 by 655 ft).

Health

The best way to care for your horse's health is to register with a veterinarian. The veterinarian will give your horse regular check-ups. At the same time, they will give you the best advice on food and exercise.

Horses often hide their discomfort, so watch closely for changes in your horse's manner or any unwillingness to be tacked up.

Vet Time

A veterinarian will give your horse vaccinations that protect it from common diseases, such as equine influenza (horse flu) and tetanus. The vet will also give worm treatments, which prevent intestinal worms from living in your horse's belly. Ask the vet to check the fit of your horse's saddle and bridle, as poor fit is a common cause of discomfort. Discuss your horse's daily and weekly exercise routine to make sure it is neither too much nor too little for their health and age.

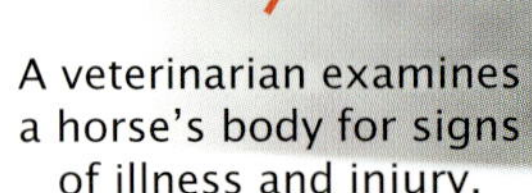

A veterinarian examines a horse's body for signs of illness and injury.

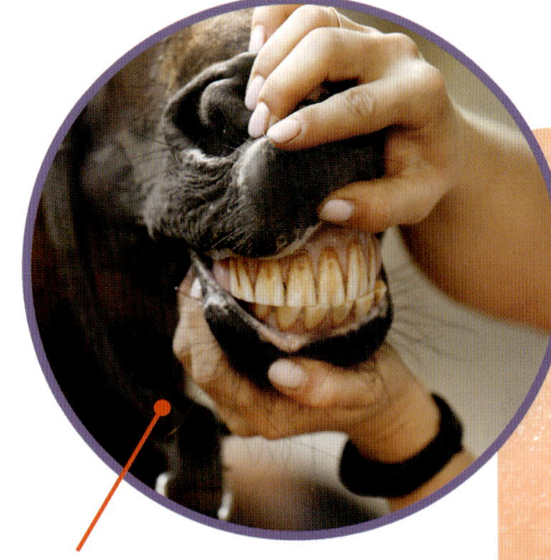

Young horses have 24 "baby" teeth, which fall out—like a human child's teeth—as their permanent teeth grow. Fully grown mares have 36-40 teeth, while mature males have 40-42 teeth.

Tooth Care

Your horse's teeth need regular checks, just like yours do! Tooth problems can cause pain, difficulty eating, tooth loss, and problems with the bit (the portion of a horse's tack that contacts their mouth). A veterinarian or qualified horse dental technician will check for tooth decay, cracks, and disease. They may use a tool called a rasp to remove sharp edges and the overgrowth of particular teeth.

AMERICAN QUARTER HORSE

Height: 14–16 hands (142–163 cm; 56–64 in)
Lifespan: 25–30 years
Origin: United States
Coat: All coats, including spotted, but the most common shade is chestnut
Uses: Family and Western riding, racing, hunter competitions, dressage, showing, and ranch work
Personality: Intelligent, easy to train, and friendly

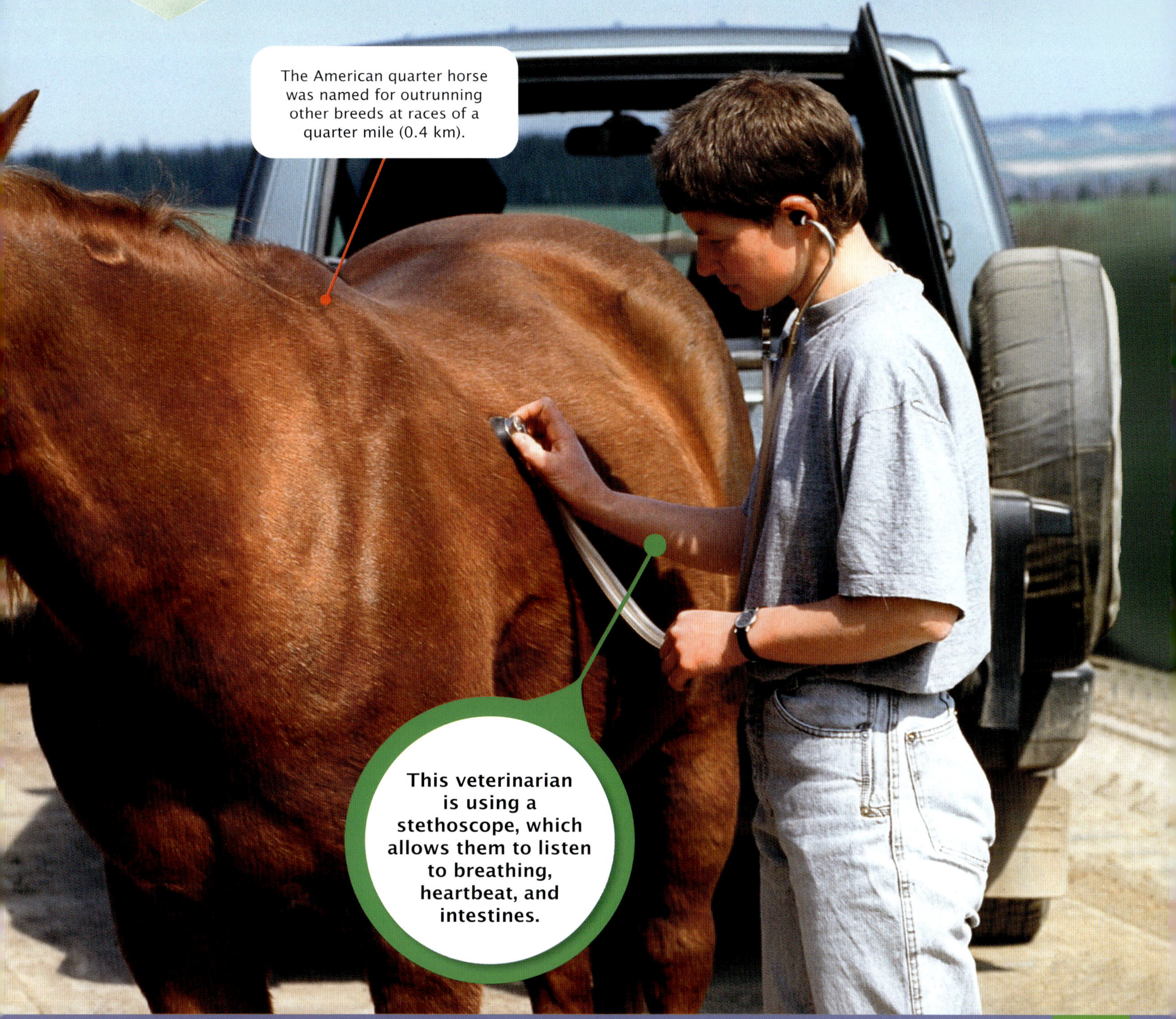

The American quarter horse was named for outrunning other breeds at races of a quarter mile (0.4 km).

This veterinarian is using a stethoscope, which allows them to listen to breathing, heartbeat, and intestines.

DID YOU KNOW? Take your horse's temperature regularly to make sure it is around 37–38.5 °C (99–101.5 °F), then call your veterinarian if it rises or falls.

Chapter 3

Heavy Horses

Usually weighing more than 640 kg (1,400 lb), these horses may also be called draft (also spelled draught) horses or coldbloods. They were bred for hard work, from pulling farm equipment to towing barges. While some heavy horses still work on small farms, most are now used for riding or showing.

The Suffolk punch was named for the English county of Suffolk and an old English word for "stout."

Powerful Body

Heavy horses have been bred to be large: usually more than 16 hands (163 cm; 64 in) high at the withers. They also have a broad body, strong muscles, and thick bones. In comparison with a race horse, their limbs are short and wide. All these qualities give the strength to exert great pulling power at low speed.

This Postier Breton horse has a muscular body and stout legs with broad joints. It was bred in the 19th century to pull mail coaches.

SUFFOLK PUNCH

Height: 16.1–17.2 hands (165–178 cm; 65–70 in)
Lifespan: 25–30 years
Origin: England
Coat: Always chestnut
Uses: Bred for farming; now used for shows, advertising, and forestry
Personality: Determined, hard-working, and intelligent

Coldbloods

These horses are called "coldbloods" for two reasons: their temperament and the climate of the cool region of northern Europe where many were bred. In terms of temperament, these horses are not sensitive and speedy like a "hotblooded" race horse. They are usually patient and gentle. If treated kindly, they can be relied on to complete the job at hand.

DID YOU KNOW? A heavy horse needs to drink up to 95 liters (25 US gallons)—or 380 glasses—of water every day.

Shire

The tallest of all horse breeds, the Shire was bred in the English "shires" of Lincolnshire, Leicestershire, and Cambridgeshire. This horse was once the most common breed in England. Today, fewer than 1,500 of these much-loved giants remain.

The Shire horse was bred from medieval English warhorses, which carried knights in heavy, metal armor into the thick of battle.

Before showing a heavy horse, its recently washed feathers may be coated in sawdust to help keep dirt out of the wet hair.

Feathering

Like many heavy horses, the Shire has longer hair, known as feathering, on its lower legs. This characteristic developed in the hardy British ponies from which the Shire is partly descended, as it protected their feet from both mud and brambles. To keep a Shire or other feathered horse comfortable, the feathering must be shampooed regularly, then dried completely to avoid skin irritation. To prevent knotting, use a detangling brush daily and clip the longest hair regularly. Finish with a grooming oil, which will repel mud and water from the horse's skin.

Working Horse

During the 19th century, before the invention of motorized transportation, hundreds of thousands of Shire horses were at work in Britain. They toiled in fields, pulled buses, and hauled carts holding goods, coal, garbage, and barrels of beer. A common use for Shires was pulling barges, using a tow rope as they walked along a canal-side path.

This Shire horse is demonstrating the skill of barge-pulling on England's Grand Western Canal.

DID YOU KNOW? The largest known horse was a Shire named Samson who was born in 1846, was 21.2 hands (218 cm; 86 in) tall, and weighed 1,524 kg (3,360 lb).

SHIRE

Height: 16–19.2 hands (163–198 cm; 64–78 in) and sometimes taller
Lifespan: 25–30 years
Origin: England
Coat: Bay, brown, gray, black, or roan
Uses: Bred for farming and transportation; now used for shows, riding, forestry, and delivering beer
Personality: Easy-going, gentle, and focused

The Shire horse's nose is slightly Roman, which means there is a gentle bump between the forehead and nostrils.

The size of dinner plates, the Shire's hooves are wide enough to support its great weight, which averages 1,000 kg (2,200 lb) for a stallion.

Clydesdale

This horse takes its name from the valley of Scotland's River Clyde. Here, in the 17th century, local horses were bred with Flemish heavy horses from Belgium. The resulting Clydesdale is known for its wide hooves, around 50 cm (20 in) across, which prevented it from sinking into the valley's boggy soil.

The long, fluffy hairs of this mare's "beard" help to keep her warm.

The Clydesdale is "barrel-chested," which means its jutting chest houses large lungs, giving excellent stamina.

Shoeing a Clydesdale

A Clydesdale is often given a "Scotch bottom" horseshoe, which extends beyond the outer edges of its hooves. This wider type of horseshoe gives the horse broader support. A Scotch bottom is also made from thicker steel for extra cushioning from the "shock" of its footfalls. This protects the hooves and legs of Clydesdales driven on hard road surfaces.

A Clydesdale's Scotch bottom shoes can weigh 2.3 kg (5 lb).

DID YOU KNOW? Like many other heavy horses, the Clydesdale is a slow-maturing breed, not reaching full height and weight until it is 8 years old.

The most famous team of Clydesdales is the Budweiser Clydesdales, which today take part in parades, shows, and TV commercials. The first Clydesdales started hauling Budweiser beer in the United States in 1933.

High Stepper

The Clydesdale is known for its high-stepping walk and trot, which means that the horse lifts its feet farther from the ground than most breeds. This gait was natural to some early Clydesdales, then owners encouraged it with selective breeding. The gait is impressive and elegant in horses used for parades and show driving. However, it can make riding a Clydesdale a bumpier experience.

A Clydesdale's thick—usually white—feathering can hide a leg injury, so carry out a close daily leg inspection, checking for scratches, skin problems, and hoof cracks.

CLYDESDALE

Height: 16–18 hands (163–183 cm; 64–72 in)
Lifespan: 20–25 years
Origin: Scotland
Coat: Usually bay, brown, or roan, with white on the face, legs, and feet
Uses: Bred for farming and hauling coal; now used for carriage driving, shows, and riding
Personality: Calm, happy, and easy to train

Percheron

Born in the old Perche region of northern France, the Percheron breed is famed for its good temperament: It is calm under pressure yet always willing to work. Due to its lack of leg feathering and its good skin, it is easier to care for than some heavy breeds.

The Percheron's large, intelligent eyes are set in a broad forehead.

Visible at Night

From the 17th century, horses from Perche were bred to pull stagecoaches, the long-distance buses of their day. The preferred coat for these Percherons was gray, since it was more visible at night than darker shades. To the present day, most Percherons remain gray.

Today, most Percherons are used for riding rather than night-time driving, but many still have a pale coat that can be seen at a distance.

PERCHERON

Height: 15.1–19 hands (155–193 cm; 61–76 in)
Lifespan: 25–30 years
Origin: France
Coat: Usually gray or black
Uses: Bred for transportation; now used for riding, carriage driving, and farming
Personality: Willing, intelligent, and unflappable

DID YOU KNOW? In the days when Percherons were working horses, they were known for being able to trot up to 60 km (37 miles) in a day.

Founding New Breeds

Percherons have helped to create many new breeds across the world. In Russia, for example, Percherons and Clydesdales were bred to create the Vladimir heavy horse. Percherons have also been bred with light horses to create breeds that—like a Percheron—are known for their large size and easy personality, but have a lighter horse's greater agility. In both Australia and the United States, many police horses are Thoroughbred-Percheron crosses.

North Swedish

Known as the Nordsvensk in Sweden, this is one of the smallest draft horse breeds. Despite its more compact frame and a weight of only 600–700 kg (1,320–1,540 lb), this is a strong and tireless horse.

These North Swedish farm horses have a long, muscular back and a powerful neck.

This mare and her foal belong to the stronger and heavier North Swedish farm horse line.

Two Lines

During the 19th century, the North Swedish horse was bred from native horses for working in farming and forestry. Yet the horse was soon recognized for its excellent trotting ability. During the early 20th century, some owners selectively bred for even better trotting. Eventually, two lines of North Swedish horse were established: the North Swedish farm horse and the faster, lighter North Swedish trotter, which is suited to harness racing.

Trotting Races

Trotting races are a popular sport in Sweden, held at more than 30 tracks across the country, with 3,000 drivers and 18,000 horses in training. Horses must pull a two-wheeled cart at a trotting gait. Races are usually over 1.6 km (1 mile). The horses used for the races are often the North Swedish trotter and its close Norwegian relative, the Dolehest.

North Swedish trotters race on the February ice of Sweden's Are Lake.

DID YOU KNOW? A world record for coldblood trotters—of 1 minute 18 seconds per 1 km (0.6 miles)—was set in 2005 by Järvsöfaks, who had North Swedish and Dolehest ancestry.

NORTH SWEDISH

Height: 14.1–16.1 hands (145–165 cm; 57–65 in)
Lifespan: 20–30 years
Origin: Sweden
Coat: Brown, bay, chestnut, gray, black, buckskin, or palomino
Uses: Bred for farming and forestry; now used for riding and harness racing
Personality: Easy-to-train, energetic, and reliable

As machines have taken over from animal-powered tools, the North Swedish farm horse has been added to Sweden's list of endangered breeds.

In comparison with other European heavy horses, the farm horse's smaller size was suited to working in Sweden's forests and small farms.

Brabant

Also known as the Belgian draft horse, this breed is from the old Brabant region of Belgium. Although other breeds are taller, the Brabant is the heaviest of all horses, with stallions reaching weights of up to 1,360 kg (3,000 lb).

Known for its intelligent expression, the Brabant has a small head, square jaw, and straight profile.

Roan Coat

Around 80 percent of Brabants are roan. This is when a horse has white hairs evenly spread through the base coat of its body, but much of the head, lower legs, and tail is a solid color. Common shades include blue roan (a black base coat, with the silvering creating a slightly bluish appearance) and bay roan (a brown to reddish-brown base coat).

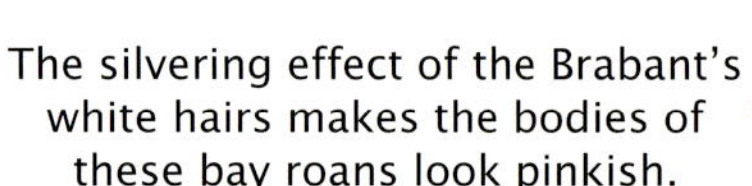

The silvering effect of the Brabant's white hairs makes the bodies of these bay roans look pinkish.

BRABANT

Height: 16–17 hands (163–173 cm; 64–68 in)
Lifespan: 20–25 years
Origin: Belgium
Coat: Usually roan, but may be bay, chestnut, gray, and black
Uses: Bred for farming and forestry; now used for riding, driving, and farming
Personality: Sensible, tough, and lively

Strong Relatives

The Brabant is closely related to other heavy horses of its region, including the Ardennais and Dutch draft. In the 19th century, breeding with the Brabant was used to make the Ardennais stronger. As a result, the average weight of the Ardennais increased from 550 kg (1,210 lb) to 850 kg (1,870 lb). The heavily muscled, tireless Dutch draft horse was developed in the early 20th century from breeding local mares with Brabant and Ardennais stallions.

The Ardennais developed in the Ardennes area of Belgium, Luxembourg, and France. It is still used in forestry due to its impressive pulling power.

The Dutch draft horse was bred in the coastal province of Zeeland, in the Netherlands. This horse's mane is braided in a traditional style to keep it clear of the harness.

This Brabant filly, named Eva, is blue roan.

The short, thick legs have moderate to abundant feathering.

DID YOU KNOW? Like other heavy horses, a Brabant will need a larger stable of around 5 m (16.4 ft) by 5 m (16.4 ft) for comfort.

Noriker

The Noriker developed in the Alps mountains, where it was bred to haul and carry goods such as gold, spices, salt, and wine through the peaks. As a result, the Noriker is smaller than most heavy horses, has a good sense of balance, and is sure-footed on uneven ground.

The human winner of the Kufenstechen is rewarded with a bracelet of flowers.

Kufenstechen

Norikers are ridden in the yearly Kufenstechen event, which has taken place since 1630 in the Austrian town of Feistritz an der Gail. The event is only for unmarried men, who must ride their Noriker bareback. The men take turns at striking a wooden barrel with an iron club. Each competitor takes up to three swipes until the barrel is destroyed.

A Noriker that is not working can have a forage-only diet, but a veterinarian will usually recommend giving a vitamin supplement to ensure the horse gets everything it needs for its health.

Feeding with Care

Like other horses, a fully grown Noriker needs at least 1.5 percent of its body weight in forage, with a total food intake of 1.5–3 percent of its body weight. A Noriker needs a diet of high-quality forage, such as alfalfa hay or grass. If a Noriker is very active, it may also need grains for extra energy. However, heavy horses have very efficient digestive systems, so—in most cases—they should be fed less per unit of body weight (kg or lb) than lighter breeds with a similar activity level. With this in mind, a Noriker's weight must be watched to avoid overfeeding.

DID YOU KNOW? The Noriker takes its name from the Roman province of Noricum, which covered most of Austria and became part of the Roman Empire in 16 BCE.

NORIKER

Height: 15.2–16 hands (158–163 cm; 62–64 in)
Lifespan: 20–30 years
Origin: Austria
Coat: Bay, chestnut, black, roan, and leopard spotted (pictured on the right)
Uses: Bred for mountain transportation; now used for family riding, trail riding on uneven terrain, and driving
Personality: Calm, brave, and resilient

American Cream Draft

Named for its cream coat, this heavy horse was bred in the US state of Iowa. All American cream drafts are descended from a cream-coated mare called Old Granny, who was born some time between 1900 and 1905.

This is a very rare breed, but its numbers are increasing as some farmers switch back to practices that do not harm the environment.

Champagne Gene

This breed's cream coat is produced by the champagne gene. A gene is a biological instruction that is passed down from parent to child. The champagne gene is dominant, which means that a horse needs to inherit the gene from only one parent to show its effects. The champagne gene dilutes (makes paler) the horse's coat, which—without the champagne gene—would be chestnut.

As a result of the champagne gene, an American cream has a cream coat, white mane, and pink skin with darker freckles and mottling.

Height: 15–16.3 hands (152–170 cm; 60–67 in)
Lifespan: 20–25 years
Origin: United States
Coat: Light, medium, and dark cream
Uses: Bred for farming; now used for farming, driving, and riding
Personality: Hardy, gentle, and easy to care for

DID YOU KNOW? The eyes of an American cream foal are pale blue at birth, but they darken to amber or hazel as it ages.

Safety around a Heavy Horse

Like other heavy horses, an American cream is a gentle giant, but owners must still take precautions to ensure they are safe around these huge animals. Always wear heavy-duty boots—with composite or steel toes—to protect your feet if they are stepped on. Teach your horse to give you plenty of personal space when you are leading or grooming.

Chapter 4

Light Horses

Light horses were bred for riding, sports, or carriage driving. They are lighter in weight and build than horses bred for heavy work. Depending on their use, light horses may be known for their speed, elegance, or trainability.

The Tersk was bred in Russia for riding and jumping. In comparison with a heavy horse, the Tersk has a short, narrow body. It has longer legs and a slimmer neck.

Body for the Job

The horses in this group have different conformations. A horse bred for racing has a lightweight body and long legs. It also has sloping shoulders and long shoulder blades, giving the shoulder muscles more movement and enabling a long stride. A long neck gives it greater balance and flexibility when running. A horse bred for carriage driving may be stockier, longer bodied, and shorter necked than a race horse, but slimmer than a horse bred to haul heavy loads.

Hotbloods and Warmbloods

While heavy horses are often known as coldbloods (see page 39), lighter horses may be classified as hotbloods or warmbloods. A hotblooded breed is known for its lively temperament and speed. It has its origins in a "hot" region, such as northern Africa or western and central Asia. However, most light horses are warmbloods. A warmblood is often the result of breeding between hotbloods and coldbloods to create a good-tempered horse that performs well in sports such as show jumping, dressage, and carriage driving.

The Dutch warmblood is highly successful in international dressage and show jumping. Its ancestors include Arabians and Dutch draft horses such as the Groningen.

A fast and sensitive breed, the pintabian is a hotblood that is descended from Arabian horses from western Asia. It was bred for its pinto coat, which is not allowed in purebred Arabians.

HANOVERIAN

Height: 15.3–17.1 hands (160–175 cm; 63–69 in)
Lifespan: 25–30 years
Origin: Germany
Coat: Usually chestnut, bay, gray, or black
Uses: Show jumping, eventing, and dressage
Personality: Intelligent, eager to learn, and calm enough for young riders

The Hanoverian horse is a warmblood that excels at show jumping.

This horse's ancestors include German coldblooded horses and hotblooded Thoroughbreds.

The Hanoverian has a compact, muscular body and long, athletic legs.

DID YOU KNOW? In 1735, the German-born King George II of Britain founded the stud farm near Hanover where the Hanoverian was first bred.

Arabian

One of the oldest of all horse breeds, the Arabian is famed across the world for its beauty. It is a hotblood with exceptional speed, sensitivity, and high spirits. Despite the Arabian's fine bone structure and relatively small size, the breed is also known for its strength.

The Arabian has a distinctive "dished" profile, which means that—when viewed from the side—the face gently dips between the eyes and nostrils.

Desert Horse

The Arabian developed in the hot, desert climate of the Arabian Peninsula, in western Asia. Native horses were probably domesticated by the region's Bedouin people around 5,000 years ago. The Bedouin selectively bred their horses to survive on little water and food, to be fast and intelligent for raiding, and to have stamina for long journeys. In this demanding region, where often human and horse could only depend on each other, the Arabian also developed a strong bond with its rider.

The Arabian is easy to recognize thanks to its long arched neck, its relatively flat croup (the top of its hindquarters), and its high tail carriage—which means its tail begins on a level with the top of its back.

Ancestor to All

Nearly every breed of light horse has Arabians among its ancestors. For hundreds of years, Arabians have been carried across the world by war and trade. Arabian blood has been used to add speed, beauty, and stamina to other breeds.

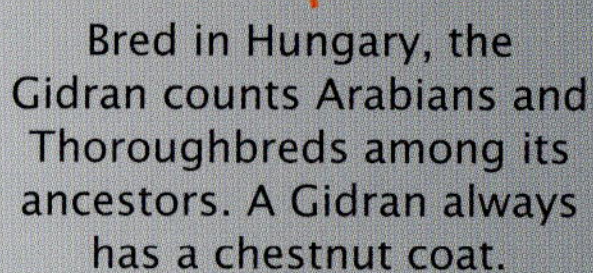

Bred in Hungary, the Gidran counts Arabians and Thoroughbreds among its ancestors. A Gidran always has a chestnut coat.

One of the Arabian's closest relatives is the Shagya Arabian, which was bred in Hungary from Arabians, with some input from European breeds such as the Lipizzaner. The Shagya is taller and less refined than a purebred Arabian.

ARABIAN

Height: 14.1–15.1 hands (145–155 cm; 57–61 in)
Lifespan: 25–30 years
Origin: Arabian Peninsula
Coat: Chestnut, bay, roan, gray, or black, with white facial markings and stockings allowed
Uses: Endurance and pleasure riding, racing, dressage, show jumping, and ranch work
Personality: Too sensitive and spirited to be suited to riders who are not experienced and patient

DID YOU KNOW? As the ancient Bedouin moved across their lands, they brought their prized and loved Arabian horses inside their tent at night to keep them warm and safe.

Barb

Also known as the Barbary horse, this hotblooded breed probably takes its name from the Berber peoples of North Africa. It was the Berber who developed this horse for riding, carrying goods, and warfare.

The Barb often has a slightly Roman nose, which means it curves gently outward.

Fantasia

Barb horses—as well as Arabians and mixes of the two breeds—take part in the horseback events known in English as fantasia but in North Africa as *mawsim* and *baroud*. In countries including Morocco and Algeria, these traditional performances take place at festivals and weddings.

During a Moroccan fantasia, the riders demonstrate their horsemanship and fire their antique rifles into the air. The performance displays the skills once used for wartime horseback charges.

BARB

Height: 13.3–15.3 hands (140–160 cm; 55–63 in)
Lifespan: 20–25 years
Origin: Maghreb region of North Africa
Coat: Usually chestnut, bay, gray, or black
Uses: Endurance and pleasure riding, dressage, fantasias, ranch work, and farming
Personality: Intelligent, quick to learn, and friendly

Crossing the World

When soldiers from North Africa invaded Spain in 711, they took their early Barb horses with them. Over the centuries, these horses influenced Spanish breeds such as the Andalusian. When the Spanish started to settle in the Americas from the late 15th century, they rode on horses of Barb and Spanish ancestry. The stamina and toughness of these horses made them well suited to their new terrain. Some descendants of those horses became a breed known as the Spanish-Barb.

DID YOU KNOW? From the Choctaw horse to the American quarter horse, most North and South American breeds have some Barb blood.

Thoroughbred

The Thoroughbred is a hotblooded breed, known for being spirited, bold, fast, and agile. Now popular across the world, the breed was developed in 17th- and 18th-century England for use in horse racing.

The Thoroughbred has a long neck and a chiselled face, with a strong, sharp bone structure.

Grooming a Thoroughbred

Like most other horses, a Thoroughbred needs to be groomed at least once a week. However, a Thoroughbred has thinner, more sensitive skin than many other breeds, so extra care should be taken. Grooming should be done slowly, avoiding any sore areas. This breed may become annoyed during grooming, so reward the horse frequently with treats and praise.

Choose a brush with softer, natural bristles rather than nylon. A rubber grooming mitt can remove mud or loose coat.

Its chest is deep and its hindquarters are powerful, which gives it extra speed and force as it gallops.

THOROUGHBRED

Height: 15.2–17 hands (157–173 cm; 62–68 in)
Lifespan: 25–35 years
Origin: England
Coat: Bay, brown, chestnut, black, gray, roan, or palomino
Uses: Racing, show jumping, eventing, dressage, and family riding
Personality: Intelligent, hard-working, but too spirited and sensitive for new riders

DID YOU KNOW? One of the fastest speeds achieved by a horse was 70.76 km/h (43.97 mph), reached by the Thoroughbred called Winning Brew in 2008.

The Anglo-Arabian is a cross between a Thoroughbred and Arabian. It has the speed of a Thoroughbred but an Arabian's greater endurance over long distances.

Three Stallions

All of today's Thoroughbreds are descended from three stallions that were brought to England from the late 17th century: the Byerley Turk, Darley Arabian, and Godolphin Arabian, which were Arabians or Turkomans (see page 68). These stallions were bred with local mares, which belonged to old breeds such as the now-extinct Irish hobby. Over the centuries since, Thoroughbreds have often been crossed with other breeds to create new ones, including the Anglo-Arabian and Irish sport horse.

The Irish sport horse is a warmblood, developed by cross-breeding the hotblooded Thoroughbred with the coldblooded Irish draught horse, which is known for its calmness.

Long legs and a lean body give this breed agility for dressage and jumping.

Cleveland Bay

In the 17th century, this horse was bred in the Cleveland region of England's Yorkshire. The breed is named for its coat, which is always bay. This uniform coloration—along with little variation in height—ensures that teams of carriage-pulling Cleveland bays are perfectly matched.

Royal Horse

In the 1920s, Cleveland bays replaced Hanoverian horses (see page 55) in Britain's royal stables, called the Royal Mews. Today, Cleveland bays regularly pull carriages containing the British royal family and dignitaries. Before starting to work in public, the horses are given training to help them remain calm among cheering crowds. The horses' manure is used to fertilize the flowerbeds in the Buckingham Palace Garden.

It is traditional for royal carriage horses to wear blinkers, which prevent them from being startled by waving flags to either side.

Heavy Warmblood

The Cleveland bay is among the old European breeds often called heavy warmbloods. Weightier than modern warmbloods, which were bred for sports, these breeds were usually bred to pull carriages. They were crosses between heavy farm or war horses and lighter, speedier horses. The Cleveland bay was initially bred from English pack horses, Andalusians, and Barbs, with some Arabian and Thoroughbred blood added later.

A pair of Gelderlanders takes part in La Venaria Reale, a traditional carriage-driving competition in Italy. The Gelderlander is a heavy warmblood that was bred in the 19th-century Netherlands to pull carriages and do light farm work.

Like most other heavy warmbloods, Hungary's Nonius has a powerful body, elegant movement, and a dark and uniform coat.

CLEVELAND BAY

Height: 16–16.2 hands (163–168 cm; 64–66 in)
Lifespan: 25–30 years
Origin: England
Coat: Bay
Uses: Driving, farming, and riding
Personality: Gentle, sensible, and easy to train

DID YOU KNOW? In the 1960s, Britain's Queen Elizabeth II saved the Cleveland bay from near extinction by buying a stallion and breeding it with purebred mares.

Gypsy Vanner

Also known as the Gypsy horse or Romani cob, this horse was bred in the British Isles by Irish Travellers and Romanichal Travellers. It is named the "vanner" because it was traditionally used for pulling caravans.

Today, few Irish and Romanichal Travellers are nomadic, yet vintage caravans and Gypsy vanners are a proud symbol of the communities' history.

Nomadic Horse

While Irish Travellers hail from Ireland and Romanichal Travellers trace their roots to long-ago India, these communities share a history of nomadism—moving from place to place. From the 19th century, these communities often lived in horse-drawn caravans. At first, caravan-owners bought and bred any strong horse, including Shire horses and native ponies such as Yorkshire's Dales pony. However, by the second half of the 20th century, a definitive breed had developed. In 1996, the first breed registries were set up, laying down standards and recording pedigrees.

The Gypsy vanner's legs are usually feathered, which is a characteristic inherited from British and Irish native ponies and heavy horses.

GYPSY VANNER

Height: 13–16.2 hands (132–168 cm; 52–66 in)
Lifespan: 25–30 years
Origin: United Kingdom and Ireland
Coat: Usually piebald, but sometimes skewbald or solid
Uses: Pulling vintage caravans, showing, riding, and dressage
Personality: Loyal, confident, brave, and easy to manage

Every June, hundreds of Gypsy vanners and more than 10,000 of their owners gather in northern England for the Appleby Horse Fair, where vanners are shown and traded. It is a tradition to take horses for a cooling splash in the River Eden.

Piebald or Skewbald

The Gypsy vanner is usually piebald, which is the British name for a pattern of white and black patches. The term comes from the black-and-white feathers of the Eurasian magpie. A vanner may also be skewbald, the British name for a pattern of white and any shade other than black. The Gypsy vanner developed these coat patterns because, in the 19th century, horses with these then-unfashionable coats were often sold cheaply, making them a sensible buy for Traveller communities.

The neck is short and muscular for pulling power and for comfort when wearing a neck collar.

The horse has strong hindquarters, with a well-rounded, broad croup.

DID YOU KNOW? The term "Gypsy" should not usually be used to describe people, but it is the name given to their horse breed by the Irish Traveller and Romanichal communities.

Marwari

This rare hotblooded horse is from the Marwar region of the state of Rajasthan, in northwestern India. The Marwari is descended from horses ridden by medieval Marwar warriors. The breed became famed for its bravery in battle.

The Marwari's face is small, delicate, and intelligent.

Extraordinary Ears

The Marwari's most noticeable characteristic is its inward-curving ears. When pricked, the tips of the ears touch each other or overlap. This unusual trait appeared naturally in a Marwari horse, and then was passed on to its descendants by careful selective breeding.

The same gene (biological instruction) that creates the Marwari's curved ears may also give it better hearing. For centuries, this horse has been renowned for hearing danger at a distance.

MARWARI

Height: 14–16 hands (142–163 cm; 56–64 in)
Lifespan: 25–30 years
Origin: India
Coat: Bay, chestnut, brown, gray, dun, or pinto
Uses: Showing, riding, dressage, and light farm work
Personality: Courageous, intelligent, spirited, and best suited to experienced riders

DID YOU KNOW? Since black is associated with death and darkness, black Marwaris are considered to be unlucky.

Kathiawari Cousin

The Marwari is closely related to the Kathiawari horse, which was bred in the nearby Indian state of Gujarat. The Kathiawari also has inward-curving ears. However, the Kathiawari is smaller and was more heavily bred with Arabian horses, giving it a dished profile and a higher tail.

Like the Marwari, the Kathiawari was bred as a desert war horse, but is today used for police work, riding, and driving.

This horse's skin is thin, which helps it stay cool in Rajasthan's hot desert. However, this makes the Marwari sensitive to skin irritations and insect bites.

Suited to maintaining speed over long distances, the legs are slender with small but sturdy hooves.

Karabakh

The Karabakh is the national animal of Azerbaijan, the country where this beautiful horse was bred. Known as the "golden horse," the Karabakh usually has a chestnut or bay coat with a characteristic golden tint.

Mountain and Steppe

For thousands of years, the Karabakh and its ancestors have been bred in Azerbaijan's Karabakh region, which stretches from the Caucasus Mountains to flat grasslands, known as steppe. The Karabakh is descended from native wild horses as well as old Asian breeds such as Kabardas, Arabians (see page 56), and Turkmenistan's Turkoman, which is now extinct but was closely related to the Akhal-Teke (see page 10). Today's Karabakh is known for its agility on mountainous terrain, as well as its stamina when racing on the steppe.

The Karabakh has thin skin and short, fine, extremely shiny hair.

Bred in the Caucasus Mountains, the hardy Kabarda puts on fat easily in summer, so it can survive hard winters.

In the 19th century, the Karabakh was used to breed the Russian Don, which shares the Karabakh's red-gold coat and its stamina.

DID YOU KNOW? In 2006, the Karabakh horse was celebrated in Azerbaijan by being depicted on a set of postage stamps.

Chovqan

Highly trained Karabakh horses are ridden by players of the ancient sport of *chovqan*. During a match, two teams of six players try to score a goal by hitting a light ball with clubs. The ball must fly into the opposing team's 3-m- (10-ft-) wide goal.

From Central Asia, *chovqan* spread to the rest of the world, where—with minor differences—it is usually known as polo.

KARABAKH

Height: 14.1–15.2 hands (145–157 cm; 57–62 in)
Lifespan: 25–30 years
Origin: Azerbaijan
Coat: Usually golden chestnut or golden bay, but may be gray or palomino
Uses: Chovqan, riding, and racing
Personality: Alert, lively, and loyal

Orlov Trotter

This Russian horse was developed in the late 18th century by Count Alexei Orlov. The count bred Arabian stallions with European mares to create a strong horse with a fast trotting gait. This made Orlov's horse a popular choice for the Russian sport of troika racing.

The Troika

The troika is a traditional Russian harness driving combination that uses three horses side by side. Unusually, the horses are driven with different gaits: The middle horse trots while the side horses canter. The middle horse, which takes a greater load, must be the strongest. The horse on the right canters by leading with its left leg, and the horse on the left leads with its right, while both horses instinctively turn their heads in opposite directions for balance.

The middle horse wears a horse collar (a padded oval that distributes the load around the neck and shoulders) and a shaft bow, which is attached to the carriage's two shafts and curves over the horse's neck. The side horses wear breast collar harnesses, which are padded straps that pass around the front of the chest, below the windpipe.

ORLOV TROTTER

Height: 15.2–17 hands (157–173 cm; 62–68 in)
Lifespan: 30–35 years
Origin: Russia
Coat: Usually gray, but may be black, bay, or chestnut
Uses: Harness racing, carriage driving, riding, and light farm work
Personality: Hard-working, gentle, and agreeable

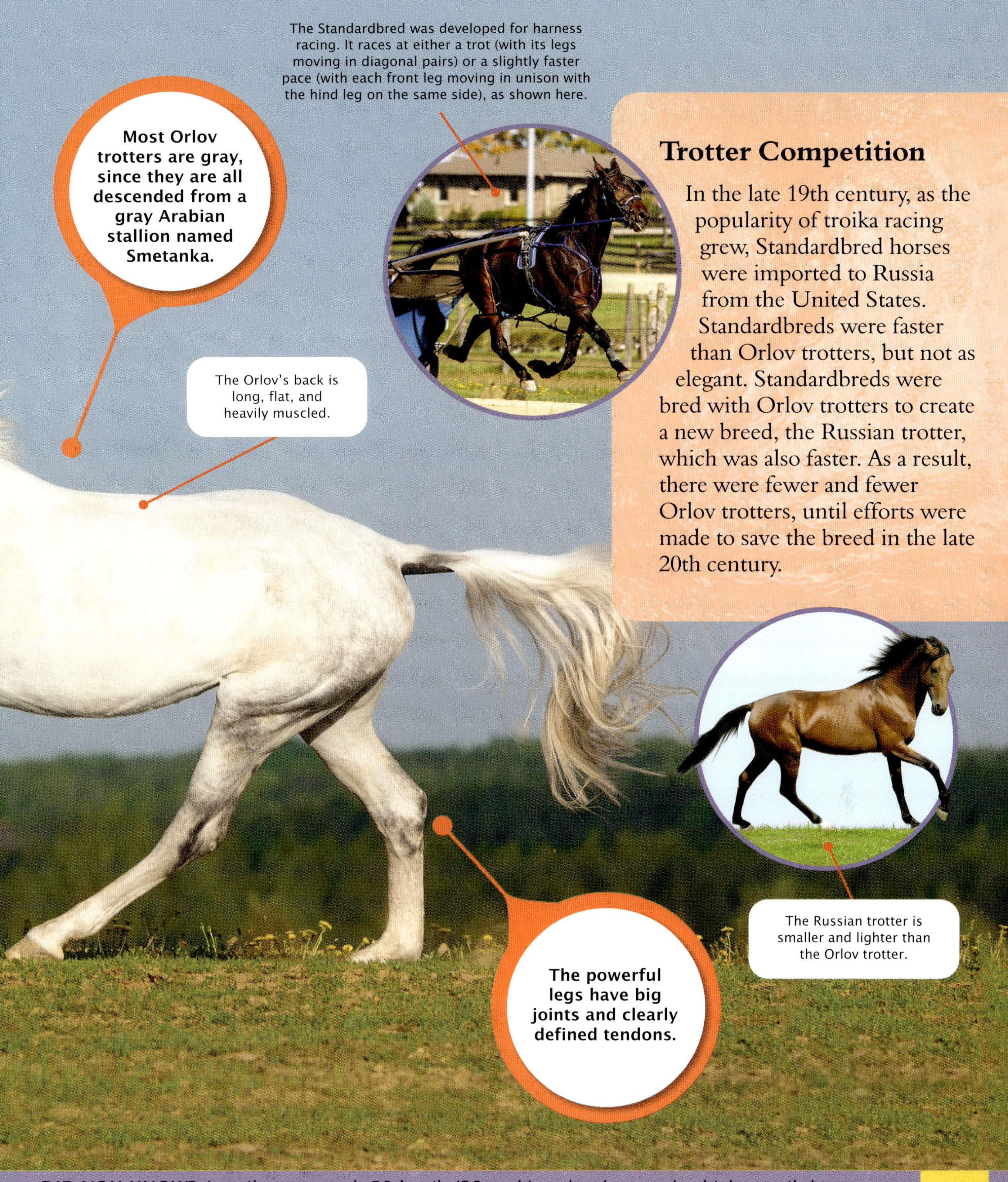

The Standardbred was developed for harness racing. It races at either a trot (with its legs moving in diagonal pairs) or a slightly faster pace (with each front leg moving in unison with the hind leg on the same side), as shown here.

Trotter Competition

In the late 19th century, as the popularity of troika racing grew, Standardbred horses were imported to Russia from the United States. Standardbreds were faster than Orlov trotters, but not as elegant. Standardbreds were bred with Orlov trotters to create a new breed, the Russian trotter, which was also faster. As a result, there were fewer and fewer Orlov trotters, until efforts were made to save the breed in the late 20th century.

The Russian trotter is smaller and lighter than the Orlov trotter.

DID YOU KNOW? A troika can reach 50 km/h (30 mph) on level ground, which—until the invention of the motor car—was considered a very fast ride.

Selle Français

One of the world's most successful sport horses, this warmblood is renowned for its excellence at show jumping and eventing. The Selle Français frequently wins medals for its riders at the Summer Olympics and World Equestrian Games.

Show Jumper

A jumping course features fences, walls, and ditches. Jumps include verticals (single fences with poles placed vertically), spreads (two sets of poles, creating a wider fence), and combinations (a series of jumps within 1–3 strides of each other). "Faults" are assessed for exceeding the allotted time, knockdowns, and refusals. Like other successful show jumpers, the Selle Français has the courage to jump tall fences and the agility to handle sharp turns and sudden bursts of speed. It also has the required height, with most medal-winners over 16 hands (163 cm; 64 in) at the withers.

The stallion Rahotep de Toscane is ridden by Philippe Rozier. Before his well-earned retirement, this Selle Français won medals including a team gold at the 2016 Rio Olympics.

Eventer

The Selle Français has the stamina, intelligence, and trust to excel at eventing. This is a competition where each horse and rider face three disciplines: dressage (see page 83), show jumping, and cross-country. Many competitions are held across three or four days, earning the name "three-day eventing."

The cross-country phase of eventing consists of obstacles—such as logs, stone walls, ponds, ditches, and banks—placed on a long outdoor circuit. A safe circuit is created by a certified designer and has fences that collapse on impact.

DID YOU KNOW? Horses are not given medals at the Olympic Games, but they are rewarded with a ribbon if their rider wins a medal.

SELLE FRANÇAIS

Height: 15.1–17.3 hands (155–180 cm; 61–71 in)
Lifespan: 25–30 years
Origin: France
Coat: Usually bay or chestnut, but may be gray or black
Uses: Competing in show jumping, eventing, dressage, combined driving, equestrian vaulting, and trail riding
Personality: Quick to learn, patient, and friendly, but some "hotter" horses may be too sensitive for new riders

A Selle Français gelding named Bentley de Sury competes with his rider Eduardo Alvarez Azmar.

The ancestors of the Selle Français include Arabians, Thoroughbreds, and native French coldbloods.

The horse's powerful, muscular legs are protected from injury by pads.

Andalusian

This breed takes its name from the Spanish region of Andalusia, where it has been bred for hundreds of years. The Andalusian is known for its strong hindquarters, compact size, and elegance. These qualities ensure this horse excels at classical and modern dressage.

First Warmblood

The Andalusian is descended from native horses of the Iberian Peninsula, where Spain and Portugal are today. Some historians say that the Andalusian was the first warmblood, since these heavier Iberian horses were cross-bred with North Africa's hotblood Barb from the 8th century. By the 15th century, the Andalusian had developed as a distinct breed.

Around three-quarters of Andalusians are gray as adults, due to a dominant gene—a biological instruction that takes effect if it is inherited from either parent. Like all gray horses, gray Andalusians are born darker, then gradually develop a paler coat.

This breed's profile is straight or very slightly dished.

Classical Dressage

The Andalusian was one of the first breeds used for classical dressage, which is an art that grew from the training of cavalry horses for the battlefield. Today, elite Andalusians are trained in classical dressage at Andalusia's Royal Andalusian School of Equestrian Art. Although classical dressage developed into modern competitive dressage, some movements are seen only in classical. These include "airs above the ground," which are movements where the horse leaves the ground.

In the capriole, the horse leaps into the air and pulls its forelegs toward its chest while kicking out with its hind legs.

For the pesade, the horse balances on its hind legs while raising and drawing in its forelegs.

DID YOU KNOW? Clint Eastwood rode Andalusian horses in many of his famous Western movies, including *High Plains Drifter* (1973) and *Pale Rider* (1985).

ANDALUSIAN

Height: 14.3–16.2 hands (150–168 cm; 59–66 in)
Lifespan: 20–30 years
Origin: Spain
Coat: Usually gray, but may be bay, black, dun, palomino, or chestnut
Uses: Classical and modern dressage, show jumping, bull fighting, and riding
Personality: Intelligent and sensitive, but gentle

Maremmano

This horse's homeland is the marshy Maremma region of central Italy. It was bred by the *butteri*, who are the horseback herders of the area's cattle. The Maremmano is known for its ability to adapt to bad weather and difficult terrain.

The Maremmano's head is long and heavy.

The Butteri

The *butteri* herd and care for the large, local breed of cattle, known as the Maremmana. Traditionally, the *butteri* wear a wide-brimmed hat for protection from sun and rain. They carry a stick called a *mozzarella* for directing the herds. Today, *butteri* still tend to herds in the Maremma Regional Park, where motorized vehicles would cause damage. *Butteri* can also be seen at local events and festivals.

The Maremmano's work with a *buttero* requires both stamina and calmness.

The Tolfetano

During the 20th century, the Maremmano horse was cross-bred with Thoroughbreds to improve its elegance. This led to the breed losing some of its hardiness. To get an idea of the Maremmano's character before it was cross-bred, we can look at its close relative, the Tolfetano horse, which was also developed for cattle-herding in the Maremmano region.

The Tolfetano is shorter, stockier, and stronger-jointed than its relative.

DID YOU KNOW? Due to its strength and courage, the Maremmano horse is now ridden by the Italian mounted police.

MAREMMANO

Height: 15.3–16.3 hands (160–170 cm; 63–67 in)
Lifespan: 25–30 years
Origin: Italy
Coat: Bay, chestnut, brown, or black
Uses: Herding, trekking, pleasure riding, light farm work, and police work
Personality: Brave, energetic, and sometimes independent-minded, making it suited to experienced riders

Lipizzaner

The Lipizzaner takes its name from the Slovenian village of Lipica, where a stud farm for the breed was established in 1580. The horse was bred for classical dressage, riding, and carriage driving. Today, this rare breed is known for its grace and skill.

Learning to Perform

Lipizzaners can be seen demonstrating their classical dressage skills (see also page 74) at Lipica Stud Farm and at the Spanish Riding School in Vienna, Austria. Although some Lipizzaner mares are trained in dressage, it is traditional for stallions to perform at these riding schools. The most capable are selected for training at the age of 4. Training takes between 5 and 8 years. Since Lipizzaners are long-lived, they often perform until the age of 25, after which they enjoy a long retirement.

The Lipizzaner is descended from horses such as Andalusians, Arabians, and Barbs.

A Lipizzaner performs a piaffe, a dressage movement in which the horse trots on the spot. This was first taught to cavalry horses, which needed to stay warm and focused while waiting to advance.

DID YOU KNOW? The 1963 movie *Miracle of the White Stallions* is based on the true story of the rescue of Lipizzaner horses in 1945, in the closing days of World War II.

Turning Pale

Although adult Lipizzaners usually look white, they are correctly called gray. Like all gray horses, they are born with darker hair and black skin. A true white horse—which is rare—is born with white hair and pink skin. Like all gray horses, the Lipizzaner has a gray gene that makes its coat turn paler as it ages. A Lipizzaner foal is usually born black or bay. White hairs appear soon after birth and become more common as the horse ages.

LIPIZZANER

Height: 14.2-15.2 hands (147-157 cm; 58-62 in)
Lifespan: 25-35 years
Origin: Slovenia and Austria
Coat: Usually gray
Uses: Classical and modern dressage, driving, and riding
Personality: Calm, co-operative, and dedicated, but often too sensitive for young riders

Frederiksborger

The Frekeriksborger was first bred by King Frederik II of Denmark in the 16th century, in the royal stud farm at Frederiksborg Castle. The king and his nobles wanted a horse that was agile, trainable, and stylishly high-stepping.

King Frederik's Horse

The Frederiksborger has an intelligent face with large eyes and generous nostrils.

King Frederik needed a handsome horse that was suitable for military parades, classical dressage, and pulling carriages. His stable managers gathered the finest horses from Europe's stud farms. These included Andalusians from Spain as well as strong, elegant breeds that are now extinct, such as Norfolk trotters from England and Neapolitans from Italy.

The Frederiksborger has a powerful neck, strong shoulders, and broad hindquarters.

Usually with a black coat and leg feathering, the Friesian was bred in the Netherlands.

Baroque Horse

The Frederiksborger is one of the Baroque horse breeds, which were popular among the wealthy during the Baroque period of European history, from 1600 to 1750. Other Baroque breeds include the Andalusian (see page 74), Lipizzaner (see page 78), Kladruber (see page 8), Friesian, Murgese, and Lusitano. These horses were often bred from war horses for driving, riding, and classical dressage. Baroque horses have a long, thick mane and tail; powerful hindquarters; a heavy, arched neck; and a noble appearance.

Bred in Portugal, the Lusitano is a close relative of the Andalusian.

The hardy but rare Murgese was bred in southern Italy.

FREDERIKSBORGER

Height: 15.1–16.2 hands (155–168 cm; 61–66 in)
Lifespan: 25–30 years
Origin: Denmark
Coat: Often chestnut, but may be bay, buckskin, palomino, or gray
Uses: Riding, dressage, show jumping, and driving
Personality: Intelligent, friendly, and so calm that it may not care about knocking down fences when jumping

DID YOU KNOW? The Frederiksborger is Denmark's oldest pedigree horse breed due to the careful record-keeping of parents and offspring since the 16th century.

Swedish Warmblood

In the mid-19th century, the Swedish state stud farms set to work on breeding a horse for riding, driving, dressage, and jumping. The result was the Swedish warmblood: an all-rounder with a co-operative and confident nature.

The Swedish warmblood is known for being graceful and flowing in motion.

Uphill Build

Like other sport horses, the Swedish warmblood has a slight uphill build, which means its withers are a little higher than its hindquarters. This can be seen by drawing an imaginary line between the highest point of the withers and the highest point of the hindquarters. This conformation helps a horse to develop agile forelegs and powerful hindlegs.

Its uphill conformation helps a Swedish warmblood to have the necessary athleticism for jumping and dressage.

This warmblood breed was developed from Swedish cavalry horses and athletic breeds such as Andalusians, Arabians, Hanoverians, and Thoroughbreds.

DID YOU KNOW? Swedish warmblood stallions are allowed to breed with pedigree mares only if they pass a test of their gaits and jumping.

Modern Dressage

In a dressage competition, a horse performs a series of movements with minimal direction from its rider. Movements include "collected" gaits, in which—at both trot and canter—the horse arches its neck, shifts its weight onto its hindquarters, and moves in a showy and animated manner; and extended gaits, in which the horse lengthens its stride with great thrust. There are also pirouettes (complete turns in place) and half-passes (when the horse moves sideways and forward at the same time).

The stallion Amiral displays the characteristics that make the Swedish warmblood excel at dressage: its fluid, careful, and sensitive movements.

The tail is high set, which helps to give an animated appearance for dressage, driving, and showing.

SWEDISH WARMBLOOD

Height: 15.3–16.3 hands (160–170 cm; 63–67 in)
Lifespan: 25–30 years
Origin: Sweden
Coat: Usually chestnut, bay, gray, or black
Uses: Dressage, show jumping, eventing, driving, and family riding
Personality: Easy to train, responsive, and calm

Oldenburger

A tall and athletic warmblood, the Oldenburger takes its name from the Oldenburg region of Germany. The breed has produced many internationally successful show jumpers and dressage horses.

Oldenburgers through Time

From the 16th century, the Counts of Oldenburg were breeding war horses. By the 19th century, a breed today known as the Alt-Oldenburger ("alt" means old) had developed, which was popular as a high-stepping carriage horse and farm horse. After the invention of motorized transportation, the Oldenburger stud farms started to develop the modern breed—by adding Thoroughbred and Anglo-Arabian blood—so it was suited for sports.

Like other Oldenburgers, this horse has large, sloping shoulders, which encourages agility in the forelegs.

Although it is rarer than the modern Oldenburger, the Alt-Oldenburger has been preserved. Today, it is used for driving, police work, forestry, and horse-assisted therapy.

DID YOU KNOW? Oldenburger fillies are given a name starting with the first letter of their dam's (mother's) name, while colts take the first letter of their sire's (father's) name.

OLDENBURGER

Height: 16–17.2 hands (163–178 cm; 64–70 in)
Lifespan: 25–30 years
Origin: Germany
Coat: Usually chestnut, bay, brown, gray, or black, but may be tobiano pinto
Uses: Dressage, show jumping, eventing, and family riding
Personality: Friendly, brave, and willing, but more hotblooded Oldenburgers are better suited to competition than amateur riding

The Oldenburger—along with other modern sport horses—has a body frame that is rectangular rather than square. This means the horse's body length is about 10 percent greater than its height at the withers.

Broader Breed

Unlike other breed registries, Oldenburger registries allow top-quality dressage or jumping horses of other breeds—such as the Selle Français and Hanoverian—to breed with Oldenburgers. This means that a pedigreed Oldenburger can have a slightly more variable conformation and temperament than other breeds. A benefit of wider breeding is that some inherited health issues can be avoided.

The hock—the complex hind leg joint that allows agile movement and pushing off the ground for jumping—is broad and strong.

Different Oldenburger lines (descended from a particular stallion) are known for excelling in different sports. In this photo, Olympian Adrienne Lyle is riding Dimacci DC of the Donnerhall dressage line.

Holsteiner

This German warmblood is famed for its skill in show jumping and hunter competitions because of its strength, technique, and carefulness. The modern Holsteiner was developed from carriage horses of Germany's Schleswig-Holstein region.

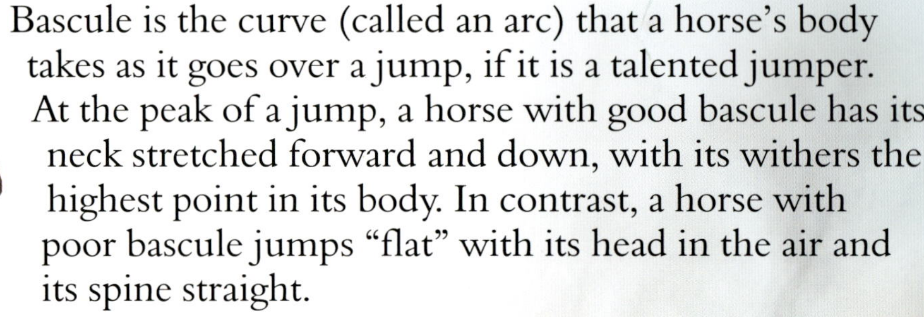

Brilliant Bascule

Bascule is the curve (called an arc) that a horse's body takes as it goes over a jump, if it is a talented jumper. At the peak of a jump, a horse with good bascule has its neck stretched forward and down, with its withers the highest point in its body. In contrast, a horse with poor bascule jumps "flat" with its head in the air and its spine straight.

The Holsteiner is renowned for its bascule, which is a benefit for show jumping (pictured) and essential for hunter competitions, as it is a quality required by judges.

Ready for competition, a Holsteiner named Lavalletto has his mane braided in the hunter style, using yarn that matches his hair.

Hunter Competitions

Often held in English-speaking countries, hunter competitions developed from England's banned sport of fox hunting. Competitions judge the skills and conformation once essential for fox hunting, without any cruelty to foxes. Depending on the competition type, horses are judged only on their appearance and gaits or also on their jumping, which is performed over walls, hedges, and fences that have a "rustic" appearance.

HOLSTEINER

Height: 16–17 hands (163–173 cm; 64–68 in)
Lifespan: 25–30 years
Origin: Germany
Coat: Usually bay, brown, chestnut, gray, or black
Uses: Show jumping, hunter competitions, eventing, dressage, and driving
Personality: Depending on the family line, calm and reliable, or sensitive and spirited

DID YOU KNOW? In the 2008 Beijing Olympics, two Holsteiners—Cedric and Carlsson vom Dach—helped to win gold for the United States show jumping team.

Appaloosa

The Appaloosa was bred by the Nez Perce, a Native American people of the northwestern United States. The horse is known for its spotted coat patterns, which are caused by a gene—a biological instruction, passed from parent to child—called the leopard complex.

Horse of the Nez Perce

There were spotted horses among the earliest horses brought to the Americas by European settlers, from the late 15th century. By 1730, the Nez Perce were breeding horses, including some with spots. A century later, the Nez Perce were selectively breeding for spotted coats, which were not only beautiful, but acted as camouflage, breaking up a horse's outline during raids and hunts. The breed's name developed from the region's "Palouse" River.

The state horse of Idaho, the Appaloosa is still bred on ranches in the northwestern United States.

This Appaloosa's hooves display the vertical stripes that are a characteristic of the leopard complex gene.

DID YOU KNOW? Prehistoric cave paintings show horses with leopard spotting, suggesting that the leopard complex gene has existed for many thousands of years.

Leopard Complex

The leopard complex gene creates coat spotting as well as striped hooves, a visible white sclera (the part of the eye surrounding the iris), and mottled skin round the eyes and lips. A horse with an unspotted coat can be registered as Appaloosa if it has these other characteristics. An Appaloosa's spotting may be in many base coat shades and in many patterns, including leopard and blanket.

APPALOOSA

Height: 14.2–16 hands (147–163 cm; 58–64 in)
Lifespan: 25–35 years
Origin: United States
Coat: Usually spotted, on a base coat of bay, chestnut, gray, black, palomino, buckskin, cream, roan, or dun
Uses: Ranch work, roping, and jumping; and Western, trail, family, and endurance riding
Personality: Gentle, versatile, and independent

Morgan

Taking its name from an 18th-century horse breeder and musician named Justin Morgan, the Morgan is one of the oldest United States horse breeds to survive to the present. The Morgan is a popular choice for both conventional and Western riding.

The Morgan horse has large, shining, and prominent eyes.

Fabulous Figure

All Morgans are descendants of a bay stallion named Figure, who was born in Massachusetts in 1789. Figure's sire (father) may have been a Thoroughbred and his dam (mother) a Thoroughbred-Arabian cross, but some historians say his parents were more workaday horses. In 1792, as payment for a debt, Figure was given to Justin Morgan. Figure was 14 hands (142 cm; 56 in) and was famed for passing on his excellent conformation and agility to his many offspring.

The Morgan has kept Figure's compact size, handsome looks, and athleticism.

Since less pressure is applied to the horse's mouth, a Western bridle may not have a noseband, browband, or even a bit. This Morgan stallion is cremello, which means it has two copies of a "cream dilution" gene, fading its chestnut coat to cream, its skin to pink, and its eyes to blue.

Western Riding

In the American West, a different style of riding and equipment developed to suit cowboys, who spent long days on horseback over rough terrain, often holding a looped rope, called a lasso, for catching cattle. A Western saddle has a bigger tree (base) for comfort, and a large pommel (front, raised area) for support and carrying a lasso. To help a cowboy ride one-handed, Western horses are trained to "neck rein," changing direction with only the touch of a rein against their neck.

MORGAN

Height: 14.1–15.2 hands (145–157 cm; 57–62 in)
Lifespan: 25–30 years
Origin: United States
Coat: Usually bay, chestnut, or black, but may be gray, roan, silver dapple, or a cream dilution such as cremello, palomino, or perlino (dilution of a bay coat; pictured on the right)
Uses: Family, Western, and endurance riding; dressage, show jumping, driving, horse therapy, and ranch work
Personality: Loyal, highly trainable, and willing

DID YOU KNOW? The Morgan was used as a cavalry horse by both sides in the American Civil War, which was fought from 1861 to 1865.

American Paint

This breed was named for its pinto coat pattern. "Pinto" comes from the Spanish word *pintado*, which means painted. An American paint horse is known both for its coat and its stock horse conformation.

This American paint horse is tovero: It has a mix of tobiano and overo patterning, with blue eyes in a dark face.

Pinto Pattern

A pinto horse has a coat with patches of white and any other shade. In the American paint horse, the other shades include black, bay, brown, chestnut, dun, palomino, buckskin, gray, and roan. The pinto markings appear in three main coat patterns: tobiano, overo, and tovero.

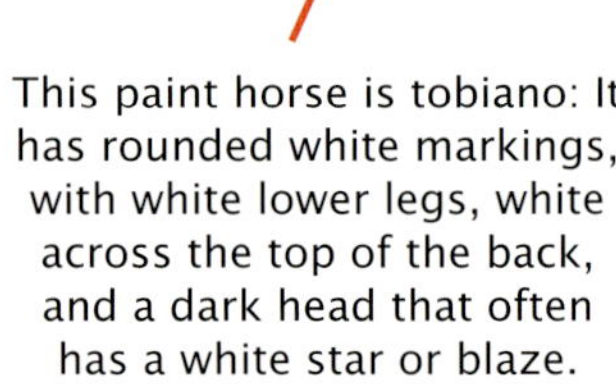

This paint horse is tobiano: It has rounded white markings, with white lower legs, white across the top of the back, and a dark head that often has a white star or blaze.

An overo horse has sharp-edged markings and is more dark than white, but it usually has a white face, sometimes with blue eyes. This paint horse has a particular pattern called frame overo: white patches on the sides of the body, leaving a "frame" of non-white.

AMERICAN PAINT

Height: 14–16 hands (142–163 cm; 56–64 in)
Lifespan: 25–30 years
Origin: United States
Coat: Usually pinto, but occasionally solid (without white spotting)
Uses: Family, Western, and endurance riding; ranch work, driving, and rodeo events such as the dangerous sport of barrel racing (riding around barrels at speed; pictured)
Personality: Easygoing, enthusiastic, and loving

DID YOU KNOW? The American paint horse is one of the fastest breeds over short distances, reaching around 64 km/h (40 mph).

Stock Horse

A stock horse has a conformation and temperament that are suited to working with cattle. Like other stock horses, the paint horse has strong hindquarters and is speedy and agile. It is also known for its "cow sense": knowing how to change its movements in response to the cattle herd, with little guidance from its rider.

The paint horse is calm and friendly around livestock.

This horse's ancestors include pinto Andalusian, Barb, and Thoroughbred horses.

Paint horses and American quarter horses (see page 36) were one breed until 1940, when the American Quarter Horse Association formed and excluded pinto horses from its registry. The American paint horse registry was founded in 1965.

Rocky Mountain

Despite its name, this breed is from Kentucky's Appalachian Mountains. The breed's name comes from a stallion brought to the Appalachians from the Rocky Mountains in around 1890. Like many of his descendants, this stallion had a chocolate coat, flaxen mane, and "single-foot" gait.

Single-Foot Gait

Instead of trotting, the Rocky Mountain horse performs an ambling gait (see page 13) called the "single-foot," because the horse lifts each foot up separately and puts it down alone. The "single-foot" is a four-beat gait: left hind, then left front, then right hind, then right front. In contrast, the trot is a bouncing two-beat gait: the left front foot hits the ground with the right hind foot, then the right front foot hits with the left hind foot.

The "single-foot" gait's extra footfalls make a journey much smoother for a rider, but allow the horse to move relatively fast for long periods over mountainous terrain.

Gaited Greats

The mountainous regions of the south-central United States are known for their gaited horse breeds, which have been selectively bred to encourage their natural tendency for comfortable-to-ride, ambling gaits. All these horses are closely related to one another.

Bred in Kentucky, the American saddlebred has a "single-foot"-like "stepping pace" and a much faster "rack" (pictured) with the same footfall pattern but different style.

The Tennessee walking horse performs a "running-walk," which has the same footfall pattern as the walk (and the "single-foot") but the hind feet overstep the prints of the front feet by up to 46 cm (18 in).

The Missouri fox trotter performs the "fox trot," in which the horse appears to walk with the front feet but trot with the back. The footfall pattern is: left front just before right hind, right front just before left hind.

ROCKY MOUNTAIN

Height: 14–16 hands (142–163 cm; 56–64 in)
Lifespan: 30–35 years
Origin: United States
Coat: Chocolate coat and flaxen mane and tail preferred, but any solid coat is allowed
Uses: Ranch work; endurance and pleasure riding, particularly for the elderly and riders with disabilities, due to the smooth ride
Personality: Calm, gentle, and loving enough for young and nervous riders

DID YOU KNOW? A Rocky Mountain horse, with rider, can perform the "single-foot" at up to 26 km/h (16 mph) over short distances.

Paso Fino

Its name meaning “fine step” in Spanish, this breed is known for its ambling gaits. Two closely related groups of horses are classed as paso finos: the Puerto Rican paso fino and the Colombian paso. Both are descended from Andalusian and Barb horses brought to the Caribbean by Spanish settlers.

The paso fino’s profile is slightly convex, curving gently outward.

Tiger Eye

Some Puerto Rican paso finos carry a gene called tiger eye. It causes the brown iris of the horse’s eye to be diluted to orange, amber, yellow, or (more rarely) blue. Tiger eye is a mutation: a random change in a gene that can be passed down to offspring.

The Puerto Rican paso fino is the only group of horses known to carry tiger eye. The gene is recessive, which means that a foal must inherit the mutation from both parents to show its effects.

PASO FINO

Height: 13–15.2 hands (132–157 cm; 52–62 in)
Lifespan: 25–30 years
Origin: Puerto Rico or Colombia
Coat: Any shade or pattern
Uses: Paso fino shows, gymkhana, driving, ranch work, trail riding, and horse therapy
Personality: Lively and willing, a trait that is often called “*brio*” (meaning “spirit” in English)

Smooth Ride

Paso finos have four-beat ambling gaits with the same footfall pattern as the Rocky Mountain horse's "single-foot" (see page 94). The paso fino performs its ambling with three stride lengths. Usually performed only in competition, the "classic fino" gait has rapid footfalls that cover as little ground as possible. Used during trail rides, the "paso corto" (short step) has a slightly longer stride and is around the speed of a trot. As fast as a canter or slow gallop, the "paso largo" (long step) has both increased stride length and faster footfalls.

DID YOU KNOW? When performing the "classic fino," the champion stallion Capuchino made up to 126 hoof beats per minute with only a 10-cm (4-in) stride length.

Peruvian Paso

This riding horse was bred for its smooth gaits, strength, and good temper. It is descended from horses brought to South America by Spanish settlers, such as the now extinct Spanish jennet, which had a natural ambling gait.

Marinera Dancer

The city of Trujillo is at the heart of the Peruvian paso region. At the yearly Marinera Festival, the traditional marinera dance is performed by Peruvian pasos, female dancers, and horsemen called *chalanes*.

The marinera is a stylized acting-out of a love story between a barefoot dancer and a *chalan*. The Peruvian paso circles the dancer elegantly, in time to music.

This breed's stamina is helped by a broad, deep chest, which houses large lungs.

Two Rhythms

Between a walk and a canter, the Peruvian paso performs two versions of a four-beat, ambling gait, with the footfall pattern of left hind, left front, right hind, right front. The "paso llano" (even step) has four equal beats in a 1-2-3-4 rhythm. The faster "sobreandando" (overwalking) has a 1-2, 3-4 rhythm, with a longer pause between the front foot of one side and the hind foot of the other side.

When performing the "paso llano," a Peruvian paso swings its shoulder to the side and its opposite foreleg outward. This unique movement is called the "termino."

DID YOU KNOW? Peruvian paso foals can be seen performing their clumsy version of the "paso llano" within hours of their birth.

PERUVIAN PASO

Height: 14.1–15.2 hands (145–157 cm; 57–62 in)
Lifespan: 20–25 years
Origin: Peru
Coat: Usually chestnut, bay, brown, gray, black, buckskin, palomino, roan, or dun
Uses: Marinera dancing and showing; trail, endurance, and pleasure riding, particularly for people who suffer from back pain
Personality: Energetic, intelligent, friendly, and easy to train

Australian Stock Horse

This horse has a strong and broad back, which helps to make it an untiring mount.

The Australian stock horse was bred for herding cattle. It has the necessary toughness and agility for long days, swift turns, and extreme weather. There are around 190,000 registered Australian stock horses, making it the country's most common native breed.

Mustering

Today, Australian stock horses are still used for mustering (rounding up) cattle, which must be done when animals are being sold, health-checked, fed, or taken to another location. Although motorbikes, quad bikes, and helicopters are used in flatter regions of Australia, horses are the only safe option in more mountainous areas.

The Australian stock horse is bred for courage, as it must stay calm among an unpredictable herd.

This stockwoman is driving her steer around the yard.

Campdrafting

The Australian stock horse is the most popular breed for the sport of campdrafting, which developed from the skills required by stockmen and stockwomen. In campdrafting, a rider must "cut out" one steer or heifer (a young male or female) from the herd of cattle in a yard, and then drive it into making two or three turns. Then the rider directs the animal out of the yard and through a figure-of-eight pegged course.

AUSTRALIAN STOCK HORSE

Height: 14–16.2 hands (142–168 cm; 56–66 in)
Lifespan: 20–30 years
Origin: Australia
Coat: Brown, bay, chestnut, gray, black, roan, pinto, dun, and palomino
Uses: Stock work, pleasure and endurance riding, show jumping, eventing, and stockman sports such as campdrafting, team penning, and cutting
Personality: Responsive, brave, and quick to learn

The face is delicate, with a broad forehead and wide eyes.

The Australian stock horse is descended from breeds brought to Australia by European settlers, including Thoroughbreds, Arabians, American quarter horses, and hardy ponies such as the Timor and Welsh mountain.

DID YOU KNOW? This breed is often ridden with an Australian stock saddle, which has a deep seat and knee pads for long hours and rough terrain.

Chapter 5

Ponies

A pony is a small horse, usually less than 148 cm (58 in) high at the withers when mature. Pony breeds are often wider bodied and thicker haired than larger horses. Many breeds are known for being tough, intelligent, and full of personality.

The Connemara region of western Ireland was the birthplace of the Connemara pony.

Definition of a Pony

According to the International Federation for Equestrian Sports, a pony is a fully grown horse that measures less than 14.2 hands (148 cm; 58 in) at the withers, without shoes on. Yet some horse experts define a pony as any smallish horse with a particular conformation: a broad body, neck, and head; a thick coat, mane, and tail; and short legs compared with its body size.

The Polish konik pony is 12.3–13.3 hands (130–140 cm; 51–55 in) at the withers. It is known for its thick dun coat.

CONNEMARA PONY

Height: 12.2–14.2 hands (128–148 cm; 50–58 in)
Lifespan: 25–35 years
Origin: Ireland
Coat: Black, gray, brown, bay, dun, roan, chestnut, palomino, or cream
Uses: Show jumping, eventing, dressage, endurance, and family riding
Personality: Calm, kind, intelligent, and easy to train

DID YOU KNOW? A 14.1-hand Connemara-Thoroughbred cross named Stroller was the first pony to compete in the Olympics, winning silver for show jumping in 1968.

Hardy and Sturdy

Small and hairy horses developed naturally in harsh climates where there is limited food. This is because smaller, hairier animals can stay warm in cold, windy places. Smaller animals can also survive on less food. This meant that bigger horses died out in those regions, but small horses survived to have foals that inherited their useful characteristics. This process—in which animals suited to their environment survive—is called natural selection. In addition, humans living in these harsh regions played a role in developing today's pony breeds. They chose the sturdiest ponies to breed with each other, ensuring that many ponies are remarkably strong for their size.

Thousands of years ago, the pottok developed—through both natural selection and selective breeding—in the Pyrenees Mountains of the Basque Country, in southern France and northern Spain. In winter, the pony's coat grows up to 10 cm (4 in) long to keep it warm.

With strong legs and a broad, well-muscled body, the Connemara is sure-footed on uneven ground and has good endurance.

The Connemara was bred from native horses and ponies brought to Ireland by the Vikings.

Shetland Pony

This pony is from Scotland's wet and windy Shetland Islands, which lie 170 km (110 miles) northeast of mainland Scotland. The Shetland was once used for pulling carts and carrying seaweed to fertilize the fields. Today, the pony is a beloved mount for children across the world.

Therapy Ponies

Due to their small size, gentle nature, and adorable appearance, Shetlands are often used as therapy animals. They are taken to nursing homes, residential homes, schools, and nurseries. Petting the ponies helps with relaxation and happiness. Talking to them may help children and adults who find communication difficult.

Pumuckel (left), Lion (middle), and Goldi (right) visit a nursing home in Germany. At only 5 hands (52 cm; 20 in), Pumuckel is one of the world's smallest ponies, even though his parents were ordinary-sized Shetlands.

Up to 14.2 hands (148 cm; 58 in), a Highland pony often has a dun coat. A foal's coat usually changes as it grows.

Scottish Ponies

Scotland was once home to many native pony breeds, but only two others have survived to the present: the Highland and Eriskay. While both are rare, the Eriskay is endangered, with fewer than 300 females remaining. It was bred to help with farming and transport on Scotland's Hebrides islands, while the larger Highland pony developed on the mainland.

Between 12 and 13.2 hands (122–137 cm; 48–54 in), the Eriskay usually has a gray coat.

DID YOU KNOW? The Shetland pony was bred with Arabian horses and Welsh and Hackney ponies to create the taller and more elegant American Shetland pony.

SHETLAND PONY

Height: 7–10.2 hands (71–107 cm; 28–42 in)
Lifespan: 20–30 years
Origin: Scotland
Coat: Any coat apart from spotted
Uses: Children's riding, horse-assisted therapy, and light carriage driving
Personality: Friendly, playful, and a little stubborn

Many Shetland ponies wander freely on the Shetland Islands, but every one of them is owned and cared for.

In winter, the Shetland pony grows a double coat, with long, waterproof guard hairs and softer, shorter hairs for warmth. This coat is shed in summer to reveal a shorter, smoother coat.

The Shetland pony has a deep girth, which means there is a large distance from its withers to its chest floor.

Welsh Mountain Pony

The Welsh mountain pony is the smallest of the four breeds in the Welsh pony and cob group. Once used in farming, warfare, and coal-mining, the mountain pony is now a popular riding pony for children and driving pony for adults.

The Welsh mountain pony has large eyes and little, pointed ears.

This pony breed has a small head with a narrow muzzle. Due to the influence of its Arabian ancestors, the pony's profile is dished (with a dip between the eyes and nostrils).

Suited to the Mountains

Over the last 3,000 years, the Welsh mountain pony developed among the mountains of Wales. The ponies were initially bred from wild native ponies, which were naturally hardy due to the harsh climate and limited shelter and food. After the Romans arrived in Britain, in 43 CE, Welsh ponies were bred with Arabian horses, making the mountain pony's conformation a little more elegant.

A herd of mountain ponies wanders free in the Carneddau Mountains of north Wales. Although the ponies are owned and given veterinary care by local families, they feed themselves on grasses, rushes, and gorse.

WELSH MOUNTAIN PONY

Height: Up to 12 hands (122 cm; 48 in)
Lifespan: 25–35 years
Origin: Wales
Coat: Any solid coat, most commonly black, gray, bay, and chestnut
Uses: Children's riding and jumping, pleasure driving, and driving events
Personality: Intelligent, spirited, and easy to train

In the Family

The Welsh mountain pony was bred with horses such as the Thoroughbred and Norfolk trotter to create three other breeds. The family now includes the Welsh mountain pony (also called "section A"), Welsh pony of riding type (section B), Welsh pony of cob type (section C), and Welsh cob (Section D). "Cob" is a British name for any stout-bodied draft pony.

DID YOU KNOW? The American Morgan horse is probably descended from Welsh cobs left behind by British forces when the Revolutionary War ended in 1783.

Icelandic Horse

Although it is often called a horse, this breed is usually the size of a pony. It is Iceland's only horse breed, descended from horses brought to the almost uninhabited island by Viking settlers from the 9th century.

An Icelandic horse needs to be groomed every day to prevent dirt building up in its thick coat, which can cause skin irritations.

Hairy Horse

Due to living in an extremely cold and windy climate for over a thousand years, this breed has developed a particularly warm and waterproof coat. Its coat is double, which means it has long waterproof guard hairs and a warm, fluffy undercoat. The coat reaches 15 cm (6 in) long in winter. As a result, the Icelandic's winter coat can be difficult to manage. A mud brush should be used to remove dirt and mud, followed by a detangler for the coarser hair. Finish with a coat oil. If an Icelandic is kept in a milder climate than Iceland, clip hair during winter to avoid sweating.

Tölt and *Flugskeið*

As well as the usual gaits—walk, trot, canter, and gallop—the Icelandic can perform a *tölt* and *flugskeið*. The *tölt* is a four-beat ambling gait (see page 13) that is comfortable for the rider but can reach the speed of a canter. The *flugskeið* ("flying pace") is a two-beat gait that can reach 48 km/h (30 mph) over short distances.

In the *tölt*, the footfall pattern is the same as the walk: left hind, left front, right hind, right front.

In the *flugskeið*, the footfall pattern is: left hind and left front; moment of suspension; right hind and right front.

ICELANDIC HORSE

Height: Usually 12–14.2 hands (122–147 cm; 48–58 in)
Lifespan: 25–40 years
Origin: Iceland
Coat: Most coats, including black, gray, chestnut, dun, bay, palomino, pinto, and roan
Uses: Herding sheep, family riding, and racing
Personality: Affectionate, adventurous, and quick to learn

Early settlers let their horses roam free in the summer, since they thought this gave the animals stronger survival skills. The tradition has continued to this day. Before winter, horses are rounded up and returned to farms.

In winter, temperatures in Iceland are around freezing (0 °C/32°F), though it can drop as low as −15 °C (5 °F).

The Icelandic horse is sure-footed, with hard hooves and short but strong legs.

DID YOU KNOW? To protect Icelandic horses from disease and interbreeding, Icelandic law has banned bringing horses into the country since the 10th century.

Gotland Pony

This pony is from the Swedish island of Gotland, which is 90 km (56 miles) east of the mainland, in the Baltic Sea. One of the world's oldest horse breeds, the Gotland is the only Swedish native pony that has survived into the 21st century.

Ancient Pony

The Gotland is descended from small horses that lived wild on Gotland from at least 4,000 years ago. Over time, many of the ponies were domesticated for riding and pulling farmers' loads. Others were left to roam the island's forests. During the 19th century, much of the forest was cut down to make room for farming, while many ponies were sold to foreign buyers. To save the breed, the first stud farms were set up in the 20th century. Female Gotlands were bred with a small number of Welsh ponies to help increase their numbers.

For thousands of years, the Gotland pony's natural home has been forest.

The Lojsta herd is supervised daily and given hay to eat in winter, when wild plants are scarce.

Running Free

To preserve the Gotland pony in a near-natural state, a herd of feral (once domesticated but then released into the wild) ponies lives on Gotland's Lojsta Heath. The herd numbers 50 animals, rising to 80 when new foals are born in summer.

DID YOU KNOW? The oldest written mention of Gotland ponies is in a 13th-century Swedish law that mentions "Gotland's wild horses."

GOTLAND PONY

Height: 11.2 to 13 hands (117–132 cm; 46–52 in)
Lifespan: 20–30 years
Origin: Sweden
Coat: Usually chestnut, bay, or dun, but all coats are allowed except roan and pinto
Uses: Children's riding, dressage, jumping, and driving
Personality: Gentle, intelligent, and full of energy

Fjord Horse

The fjord horse is an unusual combination of small size, draft-horse build, and warmblood agility. It takes its name from the long, narrow sea inlets that are a key feature of the landscape in its Norwegian home.

Descended from native horses, the fjord horse was selectively bred by the Vikings.

Two Toned

Like many ancient horse breeds, including those shown in prehistoric cave paintings (see page 8), the fjord horse is usually dun: tan to gold with a dark dorsal (along its spine) stripe and a dark mane and tail. A notable characteristic of the fjord horse is that it also has lighter hairs on the outside edges of its mane and tail, creating a dramatic two-toned look.

The fjord horse's mane is often clipped in a distinctive crescent shape so that it stands upright and emphasizes the dark central stripe.

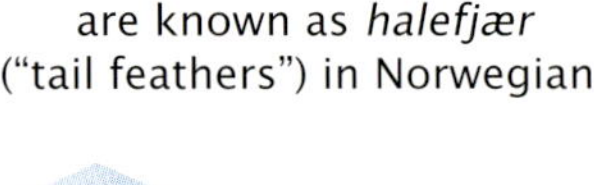

The dark hairs in the tail are known as *halefjær* ("tail feathers") in Norwegian.

FJORD HORSE

Height: 13.1–14.3 hands (135–150 cm; 53–59 in)
Lifespan: 25–30 years
Origin: Norway
Coat: Usually dun, in shades from yellow-brown to white
Uses: Riding, driving, and horse-assisted therapy
Personality: Mild, patient, and eager to please

The fjord horse's forehead is broad and flat, while its eyes are large.

The body is sturdy and heavily muscled, allowing this small horse to carry adults.

Hard Worker

The fjord horse was bred for use in war and in farming a harsh and mountainous landscape. As a result, the horse has a calm and unafraid temperament. It is also strong, but sure-footed and agile to suit its uneven terrain. Its thick coat becomes even thicker and longer in winter.

Today, some fjord horses get exercise by pulling sleighs for tourists.

DID YOU KNOW? Early fjord horses that journeyed with the Vikings may have influenced breeds such as the Icelandic horse and Scotland's Highland pony.

Skyros Pony

This rare pony breed is native to the Greek island of Skyros, in the Aegean Sea. Only around 190 of these good-natured ponies remain on the island, with around 300 more living across the world.

Made in Athens

Skyros ponies are believed to be descendants of small horses brought to the island by settlers from the Greek city of Athens, in the 5th century BCE. At that time, similar horses lived and worked across Greece, themselves the descendants of native horses that had been selectively bred. Over the centuries, the Skyros horse adapted to its rocky island home, becoming yet smaller and hardier.

The Skyros pony has long, slender nose bones and a fine muzzle.

Small horses similar to the Skyros pony can be seen in carvings from the Parthenon temple, which was built in Athens in the 5th century BCE.

Rare Pony

The Skyros is unusual among pony breeds, because—although it is pony-sized—it has a horse-like conformation. Its legs are relatively long and slender, while its body is less stout than those of most ponies. Despite being hard-hooved and sure-footed for rocky ground, it moves elegantly.

To preserve the Skyros pony, it is protected under Greek law. Organizations such as the Skyros Island Horse Trust are breeding and promoting the pony.

DID YOU KNOW? Like other ponies, a Skyros matures more quickly than a horse, reaching full size and weight at 5 or 6 years old.

SKYROS PONY

Height: 9.1–11 hands (94–111 cm; 37–44 in)
Lifespan: 25–30 years
Origin: Greece
Coat: Bay, brown, chestnut, gray, black, or dun, sometimes with stars or a dorsal stripe
Uses: Children's riding and horse-assisted therapy
Personality: Curious, friendly, and calm

Yonaguni

One of the smallest Japanese horse breeds, this pony is from the little island of Yonaguni, which is Japan's westernmost inhabited island. Until the mid-20th century, the Yonaguni carried rice and sugarcane around the tropical island.

The Yonaguni is critically endangered, with only around 130 horses remaining.

Staying Small

During the 20th century, many of Japan's native horses were bred to be larger to help with military, industrial, and farm work. Yet, isolated on its remote island, the Yonaguni was allowed to remain as small as it had been for hundreds of years.

Today, most Yonagunis are allowed to roam freely around the island, but are rounded up for veterinary visits and riding.

Mongolian Cousins

Eight native Japanese horse breeds have survived to the present. All are descendants of Mongolian horses that were taken to Japan from the 4th century. Like the Japanese breeds, which are all pony-sized, today's Mongolian horse is small—around 12–14 hands (48–56 inches; 122–142 cm)—and fairly stocky with a large head.

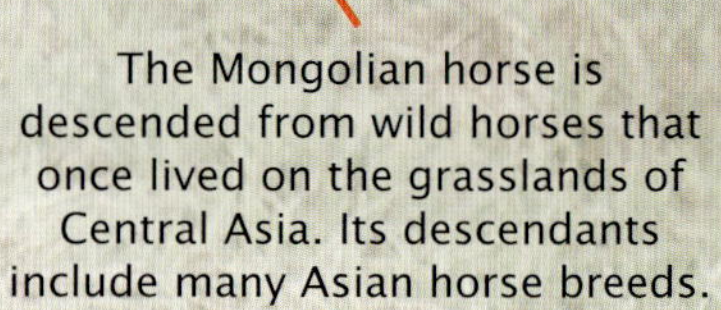

The Mongolian horse is descended from wild horses that once lived on the grasslands of Central Asia. Its descendants include many Asian horse breeds.

From the large northern island of Hokkaido, the Dosanko is the only one of Japan's native horse breeds that is not critically endangered.

Usually around 13 hands (132 cm; 52 in) and with a bay coat, the Kiso is from Honshu, Japan's largest island. Around 150 horses remain.

YONAGUNI

Height: 10.3–11.3 hands (110–120 cm; 43–47 in)
Lifespan: 25–30 years
Origin: Japan
Coat: Usually chestnut
Uses: Family riding and visiting schools and nurseries
Personality: Gentle, patient, and easy to handle

The pony's head is large with relatively small ears, while its eyes are said to be extremely expressive of its emotions.

The Yonaguni's legs are strong enough to support an adult rider. Its hooves are long and very hard.

DID YOU KNOW? Due to 20th-century breeding efforts, the largest Japanese horse breed is now the Miyako, which is around 14 hands (142 cm; 56 in) high.

Tibetan Pony

The ancestors of this hardy pony include the Mongolian horse as well as native Chinese breeds.

This pony lives on the Tibetan Plateau, a vast area of high ground that stretches over southwestern China and parts of India, Pakistan, Nepal, Bhutan, Tajikistan, and Kyrgyzstan. The pony can live at up to 4,500 m (14,800 ft) above sea level.

The Tibetan pony is usually a working animal that helps farmers and herdspeople.

The High Life

On the high-altitude Tibetan Plateau, the air is thin, with less oxygen to breathe than at sea level. Thanks to both natural selection and selective breeding, Tibetan ponies have deep chests and large lungs to take in as much oxygen as possible. Like other high-altitude animals, their blood cells are particularly efficient at carrying oxygen around the body.

To pick their way over mountainous terrain, Tibetan ponies are sure-footed and have strong legs and joints.

DID YOU KNOW? From 1,300 years ago, markets were set up in southwestern China to trade tea grown in China's Yunnan region for Tibetan ponies needed by the Chinese army.

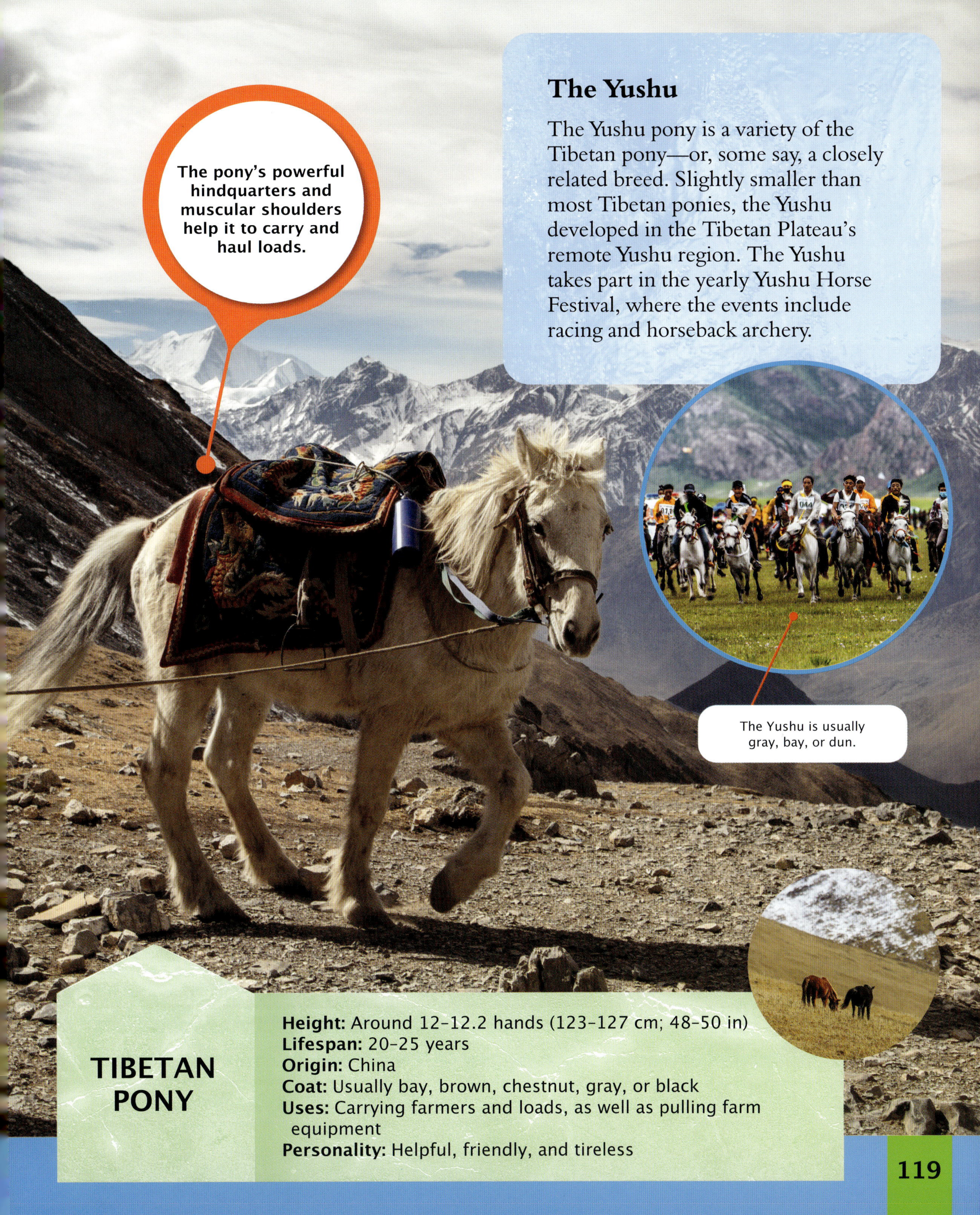

The Yushu

The Yushu pony is a variety of the Tibetan pony—or, some say, a closely related breed. Slightly smaller than most Tibetan ponies, the Yushu developed in the Tibetan Plateau's remote Yushu region. The Yushu takes part in the yearly Yushu Horse Festival, where the events include racing and horseback archery.

The Yushu is usually gray, bay, or dun.

TIBETAN PONY

Height: Around 12-12.2 hands (123-127 cm; 48-50 in)
Lifespan: 20-25 years
Origin: China
Coat: Usually bay, brown, chestnut, gray, or black
Uses: Carrying farmers and loads, as well as pulling farm equipment
Personality: Helpful, friendly, and tireless

American Miniature Horse

Although it is pony-sized, this breed is known as a miniature horse because it was developed to have the conformation of a horse rather than a pony. Unlike a pony, the American miniature has relatively long legs and a compact body.

Many Ponies

The American miniature horse was bred in the United States in the first half of the 20th century. Its ancestors probably include ponies that had worked in American coal mines. These long-suffering ponies were usually imported from Britain and may have been Shetland, Welsh, and Dartmoor ponies.

The American miniature often has the appearance of a miniature Arabian horse, with a dished profile, slender neck, and slim legs.

The American miniature has large eyes in a pretty and delicate face.

DID YOU KNOW? Ancestors of the American miniature include ponies bred by English horse-loving sisters Lady Estella and Lady Dorothea Hope in the early 20th century.

Many Coats

Due to their mixed heritage, American miniatures have coats of many shades and markings. In contrast to other breeds, all coats are accepted by registries, including markings that are uncommon among other horses.

AMERICAN MINIATURE HORSE

Height: Up to 9.2 hands (97 cm; 38 in)
Lifespan: 25–35 years
Origin: United States
Coat: Any
Uses: Children's riding, light driving, horse-assisted therapy, and companionship
Personality: Sweet, friendly, and determined

Falabella

The Falabella is the world's littlest horse breed. With its small frame, it is too delicate to be ridden, but may be kept as a pet if it is given plenty of exercise, playtime with other ponies, and suitable shelter.

Smaller by Nature

The Falabella's ancestors were small horses that developed naturally in Argentina, after Andalusian horses were brought by Spanish settlers in the 16th century. When the earliest Spanish settlements were abandoned, some horses were left to fend for themselves on the grassland. The hardy breed that developed from these feral horses is known as the Criollo. By the 19th century, some Criollos were living in isolated areas with only a small number of other horses to breed with. These Criollos had become much smaller than their ancestors.

Full-size Criollos are the traditional mount of the gauchos (cowboys) of Argentina. A Criollo can cope with extremes of heat and cold, little water, and feeding only on dry grasses.

This Falabella stallion has a rare leopard-spotted coat.

FALABELLA

Height: 6.1–8.2 hands (63–86 cm; 25–34 in)
Lifespan: 25–35 years
Origin: Argentina
Coat: Usually bay, brown, or black, but occasionally pinto, palomino, or leopard
Uses: Companionship
Personality: Curious, energetic, and playful

The Falabella Family

In 1845, a herd of small Criollos was adopted by farmer Patrick Newtall. After Newtall's death, the herd was passed to his son-in-law, Juan Falabella, who began to breed the horses with small Thoroughbreds as well as Shetland and Welsh ponies. As the Falabella family cared for the herd over several generations, the Falabella pony emerged.

Falabella foals are known for being very playful and sociable.

The Falabella's profile is slightly dished or straight.

Often said to resemble a miniature Thoroughbred, the Falabella has a slim body and fine legs.

DID YOU KNOW? After becoming extinct in the Americas around 10,000 years ago, horses returned to the continent with European explorers and settlers from 1493.

Australian Pony

Agile but tough, the Australian pony was bred to suit the extremes of climate on the Australian continent. The pony is known for its good nature, long stride, and smooth movement.

First Horses

Horses evolved in North America long after the continent of Australia was separated by a vast ocean. The first horses did not reach Australia until 1788, when they arrived with British settlers. In 1803, Timor ponies were first shipped around 740 km (460 miles) from Indonesia to Australia. It was these strong, athletic ponies that were the beginnings of the Australian pony breed.

The Australian pony has large, dark eyes; its ears are small; and its nostrils are large.

On the island of Timor, the Timor pony is used for herding cattle, light farm work, and driving.

Until 2005, the Australian pony could be bred with other breeds, but now the studbook is "closed" to keep the pony's quality.

DID YOU KNOW? The Timor pony is also the foundation breed of the Coffin Bay pony, which lives semi-wild in a large fenced area in South Australia's Coffin Bay.

The pony's neck is slightly more crested than some other breeds. The crest is the upper ridge of the neck, formed from fat and tough tissue, from which the mane grows.

The Exmoor pony is a very old breed that developed—probably from both wild and domesticated horses—on moorland in southwest England.

Developing the Breed

To create today's Australian pony, Timor ponies were bred with hardy British horses including Welsh mountain (see page 106), Exmoor, and Hackney ponies. Hotblood horses, including small Arabians and Thoroughbreds, were added to the mix.

In the 19th century, the Hackney pony was bred in England to pull light carriages. It is known for being able to trot at speed for long periods.

AUSTRALIAN PONY

Height: 11–14 hands (112–142 cm; 44–56 in)
Lifespan: 25–35 years
Origin: Australia
Coat: Usually gray but may be bay, brown, chestnut, black, palomino, or dun
Uses: Children's riding, dressage, eventing, show jumping, and gymkhana
Personality: Patient, sensible, and alert

Glossary

AMBLING GAIT
Any four-beat gait (with the four hooves striking the ground separately) that is faster than a walk but usually slower than a canter.

BAY
A reddish-brown to brown coat with black points.

BREED
A group of animals that have been selectively bred to have a particular appearance, abilities, and personality.

BUCKSKIN
A gold to tan coat with black points.

CANTER
Faster than a trot and slower than a gallop, the canter is a three-beat gait. The footfall pattern may be: left hind leg, right hind with left front leg, then right front leg.

CAVALRY
A group of soldiers who fight on horseback.

CHESTNUT
A reddish to brown coat with a similar mane and tail.

COB
A British name for any stout-bodied draft pony.

COLDBLOOD
A large, heavy horse with a calm temperament.

CONFORMATION
A horse's body shape, proportions, and muscling.

CONVEX
Curving outward.

CREMELLO
A pale cream coat, coupled with blue eyes and pink skin.

CROUP
The highest part of the hindquarters, from hip to tail.

DILUTE
In reference to a horse's coat, to make paler.

DISHED PROFILE
With a gentle dip between a horse's eyes and nostrils.

DOMESTICATED
Trained—and adapted over time—to live and work with humans.

DORSAL STRIPE
A stripe along the backbone from the withers to the base of the tail.

DRAFT (ALSO SPELLED DRAUGHT) HORSE
A horse bred for pulling heavy loads or working on farms.

DUN
A gold to gray coat with darker markings, including a dorsal stripe.

ENDURANCE
The ability to cope with long journeys or heavy work.

EVOLVE
To change gradually over time.

FAMILY
A scientific group that includes species of living things that are similar to each other.

FEATHERING
Longer hair on the lower legs.

FERAL
A domesticated animal that has escaped or been released into the wild, where it roams freely.

FLAXEN
Golden blond, usually seen in the mane and tail.

FOAL
A horse under one year old.

FORAGE
The eatable parts of plants, such as hay, straw, and grass.

GAIT
The pattern of steps that a horse uses at a particular speed.

GALLOP
A horse's fastest gait, the gallop has four beats. The footfall pattern may be: right hind leg, left hind leg, right front leg, left front leg.

GENE
Passed from parents to offspring, genes are instructions for a living thing's appearance and function. Genes are in cells, which are the building blocks of all living things.

GRAY (ALSO SPELLED GREY)
A gray horse is born with a coat of any shade, but its hairs turn white as it ages.

GRAZE
To feed on grassland.

HABITAT
The natural home of an animal, plant, or other living thing.

HAND
A measurement of a horse's height, equal to 4 inches (around 10 cm). *See also* page 5.

HARDY
Able to cope with harsh conditions.

HEAVY HORSE
A large horse bred for heavy work.

HOTBLOOD
A light horse, usually from northern Africa or Asia, that was bred for speed and spirit.

LIGHT HORSE
A horse bred for riding, sports, or swift transportation.

MARE
A female horse aged four or older.

NATIVE
Originating in that place rather than brought from somewhere else.

NATURAL SELECTION
The process through which animals better suited to their environment tend to survive, and then pass on their characteristics to their babies.

PACE
Faster than a trot, the pace is a two-beat gait with the footfall pattern: left front with left hind leg, then right front with right hind leg.

PACK HORSE
A horse used to carry goods on its back.

PALOMINO
A yellow to tan coat with flaxen points.

PARASITE
A living thing that lives in or on another living thing.

PASTURE
A field of grass and eatable herbs.

PEDIGREE
A record of a horse's parents, grandparents, and other ancestors.

PINTO
Also known as parti-colored or piebald, a coat with large patches of white over any base coat.

POINTS
When referring to a horse's coat, the mane, tail, lower legs, and ear rims.

PONY
A fully grown horse that measures less than 14.2 hands (148 cm; 58 in) at the withers.

PREY
An animal that is killed by another animal for food.

PROFILE
The outline of a horse's face, seen from the side.

PUPIL
The opening in an eye that lets in light. Light bounces off objects and into the eye, where it stimulates cells that message the brain.

ROAN
From birth, a roan horse has a scattering of white hairs in its coat.

ROMAN NOSE
A nose that curves outward, when seen from the side.

SELECTIVE BREEDING
The process of choosing which animals to breed together, so that they will pass on particular characteristics to their foals.

SILVER DAPPLE
A chocolate or gray coat with dapples (rings of paler hair) and a silver or flaxen mane and tail.

SPECIES
A group of living things that look similar and can make babies together.

STALLION
A male horse, aged four or older, that is able to father foals.

STAMINA
The ability to be active for long periods of time.

STAR
A white marking between or above the eyes.

STOCK HORSE
A horse that is suited to working with cattle.

STOCKY
Broad and strongly built.

STUD FARM
A farm where horses are bred.

SURE-FOOTED
Able to walk easily on uneven ground.

TROT
Faster than a walk but slower than a canter, the trot is a two-beat gait. The footfall pattern is left front with right hind leg, then right front with left hind leg.

VIKINGS
Scandinavian seafarers who raided and settled across Europe from the 8th to 11th centuries.

WALK
A horse's slowest gait, the walk has four beats. The footfall pattern is left hind leg, left front leg, right hind leg, right front leg.

WARMBLOOD
A horse bred from hotbloods and coldbloods to create a good-tempered sport horse.

WITHERS
The ridge on a horse's back, between its shoulders.

Index

Akhal-Teke 10–11, 68
Alt-Oldenburger 84
ambling gaits 13, 94, 96–97, 98–99, 108
American Belgian draft 39
American cream draft 52–53
American miniature 120-121
American paint 92–93
American quarter horse 36–37
American saddlebred 94
Andalusian 74–75
Anglo-Arabian 61
Appaloosa 88–89
Arabian 56–57
Ardennais 49
Australian pony 124–125
Australian stock horse 100–101

Barb 58–59
Baroque horses 80
bascule 86
bay coats 18, 55, 62–63, 77, 87
black coats 18, 41, 66, 80
Black Forest 35
Brabant 48–49
breeding and registries 5, 8, 9, 85, 103
brumbies 22
buckskin coats 10–11, 18
Budyonny 30

Camargue 23
campdrafting 100
Canadian warmblood 5
canter 12
carriage driving 24, 62, 84
chestnut coats 18, 25, 37, 38–39, 81, 117
chovqan 69
Cleveland bay 62–63
Clydesdale 34, 42–43
coats 18–19, 28–29, 108
coldbloods *see* heavy horses
communication 16–17
conformation 10–11, 38, 54, 82, 85, 102
Connemara pony 102–103
cream coats 18, 52–53, 90
Criollo 122

domestication 8
Dosanko 116
draft horses *see* heavy horses
dressage 25, 74, 78, 83, 85
driving 24, 43, 46, 62, 64, 70, 71, 84, 113
dun coats 6–7, 9, 18, 27, 102, 112–113
Dutch draft 49
Dutch warmblood 54

ears 14, 76–77
Eriskay pony 104
eventing 72
evolution 7
exercise 30, 34–35, 36
Exmoor pony 125
eyes 14, 52, 96

Falabella 122–123
farming 39, 47
feathering 40, 43, 49, 64–65
feral horses 22–23, 110
fjord horse 112–113
flehmen response 14–15
foals 20–21
food 30–31, 34, 35, 50
Frederiksborger 80–81
Freiberger 33
Friesian 80

gaits 12–13, 43, 71, 94–99, 108
gallop 12
Gelderlander 62
Gidran 56
Gotland pony 110–111
grade horses 5
gray coats 18, 54, 70–71, 74, 79
grooming 28–29, 40, 60, 108
Gypsy vanner 64–65

Hackney pony 125
Haflinger 29
hands 5
Hanoverian 55
harness racing 24, 46, 70, 71
heavy horses 33, 34, 35, 38–53
Heck 8–9
Highland pony 104
Holsteiner 86–87
hooves 7, 26, 42
hotbloods 10–11, 54, 56–61, 66–69
hunter competitions 86

Icelandic 108–109
Irish sport horse 61

Kabarda 68
Karabakh 68–69
Kathiawari 67
Kinsky 14–15
Kiso 116
Kladruber 8
Knabstrupper 21
konik pony 102

light horses 4–5, 8, 10–15, 18–31, 36–37, 54–101
Lipizzaner 78–79
Lusitano 80

Mangalarga marchador 12–13
Maremmano 76–77
markings 19
Marwari 66–67
Missouri fox trotter 94
Mongolian 116
Morgan 90–91
Murgese 80
mustang 22–23

New Forest pony 17
Nonius 62
Noriker 50–51
North Swedish 46–47

Oldenburger 84–85
Orlov trotter 70–71

pace 13, 71
palomino coats 18, 101, 107, 109, 122
Pampa 18–19
paso fino 96–97
pasture 30, 34–35
Percheron 44–45
Peruvian paso 98–99
piebald *see* pinto coats
pintabian 54
pinto coats 18–19, 54, 59, 65, 92–93, 120–121
police horses 45, 67
ponies 9, 17, 102–125
Postier Breton 38
pottok 103
Przewalski's horse 6–7

racking horse 13
roan coats 18, 48, 49
Rocky Mountain 94–95
Russian Don 10, 68
Russian trotter 71

safety 24, 53
Selle Français 72–73
senses 14–15
Shagya Arabian 56
Shetland pony 104–105
Shire 40–41
shoes 26, 42
show jumping 54, 55, 72, 73, 86
silver dapple coats 95, 121
skeleton 11
skewbald *see* pinto coats
Skyros pony 114–115
sleeping 32
socializing 16–17, 21, 26, 27, 32, 34
Sorraia 27
Spanish-Barb 59
sports 24–25
spotted coats 18, 21, 51, 88–89, 120–121, 122–123
stables 32–33
Standardbred 13, 71
stock horses 76–77, 92–93, 100–101
Suffolk punch 38–39
Swedish warmblood 82–83

teeth 36
Tennessee walking horse 94
Tersk 54
therapy, horse-assisted 4, 104
Thoroughbred 45, 60–61
Tibetan pony 118–119
Timor pony 124
Tolfetano 76
Trakehner 30–31
trot 12, 13, 46
trotting races 46, 70–71

veterinarians 24, 30, 36–37
Vladimir 45

warmbloods 54
washing 29
water 26, 34, 39
welfare 15, 24, 26, 30, 32, 34, 36–37
Welsh mountain pony and family 106–107
Western riding 90
Westphalian 24–25
whiskers 15
Wielkopolski 4–5
wild horses 6–7, 8
withers 5, 10

Yonaguni 116–117
Yushu pony 119

zebras 6